SINGLE OR JOINT VENTURING?

For Lizette

Single or Joint Venturing?

A comprehensive approach to foreign entry mode choice

JOHN BELL
Department of Business Administration
Tilburg University

Avebury

Aldershot • Brookfield USA • Hong Kong • Singapore • Sydney

© J. H. J. Bell 1996
Reprinted 1997

All rights reserved. No part of this publication may be reproduced, stored in a retrieval system, or transmitted in any form or by any means, electronic, mechanical, photocopying, recording or otherwise without the prior permission of the publisher.

Published by
Avebury
Ashgate Publishing Limited
Gower House
Croft Road
Aldershot
Hants GU11 3HR
England

Ashgate Publishing Company
Old Post Road
Brookfield
Vermont 05036
USA

British Library Cataloguing in Publication Data

Bell, John
 Single or joint venturing? : a comprehensive approach to foreign entry mode choice
 1. Foreign licensing agreements 2. International trade
 I. Title
 338 . 8 ' 8

 ISBN 1 85972 383 7

Library of Congress Catalog Card Number: 96-84694

A grant was received from the Nederlandse Organisatie voor Wetenschappelijk Onderzoek (NWO) for the language correction
Printed and bound by Athenaeum Press, Ltd.,
Gateshead, Tyne & Wear.

Contents

List of tables and figures   vii

Acknowledgements   xi

1 Introduction

1.1 Problem formulation   4
1.2 Structure of the book   5

2 Literature review

2.1 Corporate strategy and the choice of entry mode   7
2.2 Possible modes of entry   10
2.3 Theories on international business   13
2.4 A comparative analysis of theories   25
2.5 Empirical studies   30
2.6 Conclusions   39

3 Conceptual framework and hypotheses

3.1 Conceptual framework   43
3.2 Hypotheses   48
3.3 Conclusions   60

4 Methodology

4.1	Data collection	63
4.2	Variables	65
4.3	Sample	75
4.4	Statistical techniques	78
4.5	Conclusions	86

5 Results

5.1	Non-response analysis	89
5.2	Confirmatory factor analysis	90
5.3	Binomial logit analysis	99
5.4	Multinomial logit analysis	113
5.5	Ordered logit analysis	120
5.6	Conclusions	123

6 Conclusions

6.1	Conclusions	127
6.2	Implications of the results	131
6.3	Suggestions for further research	132

Appendix A Questionnaire   135

Appendix B List of host countries   157

List of references   159

List of tables and figures

Table 2.1	Overview of the findings of the empirical studies which focused on the choice between JVs and WOSs	32
Figure 3.1	Schematic presentation of the ability of theoretical approaches to provide explanations for foreign entry mode choice (JVs versus WOSs)	46
Figure 3.2	The conceptual framework of the comprehensive eclectic theory of the foreign entry mode choice	47
Figure 3.3	The four groups of variables that influence the foreign entry mode choice	59
Table 3.1	Overview of the hypothesized effects of the variables on the choice between a JV and a WOS	60
Figure 4.1	Confirmatory factor analytic model	80
Figure 5.1	CFA maximum likelihood estimates of *global strategy* and *level of competition*	91
Figure 5.2	CFA maximum likelihood estimates of *industry growth* and *cultural difference*	92
Figure 5.3	CFA maximum likelihood estimates of *international experience*	93

Figure 5.4	CFA maximum likelihood estimates of *host country experience* and *reputation*	94
Figure 5.5	CFA maximum likelihood estimates of *specific assets* and *risk of opportunism*	95
Figure 5.6	CFA maximum likelihood estimates of *host country risk*	96
Figure 5.7	CFA maximum likelihood estimates of *host government policy*	97
Figure 5.8	CFA maximum likelihood estimates of *level of welfare*	98
Table 5.1	Overview of the reliability and validity of the constructs, and of the evaluation criteria of the CFA models	99
Table 5.2	Means, standard deviations, and the correlation matrix of the dependent variable and the independent variables	100
Table 5.3	Binomial logit estimations of the eclectic model: JVs vs. WOSs	103
Figure 5.9	Effect of cultural differences on the likelihood of JVs	107
Table 5.4	Classification table of the binomial logit analysis	109
Table 5.5	Binomial logit estimations of the separate theories: JVs vs. WOSs	110
Table 5.6	Model-χ^2's, degrees of freedom, classification rates for all possible models, and a comparison with this study's eclectic model	112
Table 5.7	The number of minority, 50/50, and majority JVs based on the division of equity and the division of control	113

Table 5.8	Multinomial logit model with JVs grouped according to the level of equity	114
Table 5.9	Multinomial logit model with JVs grouped according to the level of control	119
Table 5.10	Ordered logit estimations with JVs grouped on the level of equity and on the level of control	121
Table 5.11	Comparison of the logit models: binomial, multinomial, and ordered	124

Acknowledgements

This book could only have been written because of the support and advice I obtained from a large number of people. At this place, I want to express my gratitude to all of them. First, I would like to thank my wife Lizette for all her support, patience, love, and understanding throughout the trajectory of writing this book. Harry Barkema and Alain Verbeke also contributed very substantially to the completion of this book, both with regard to the contents and the style of writing. In spite of many other time-consuming activities, they were continuously prepared to read and comment the chapters very quickly.

Furthermore, I would like to thank Sytse Douma, John Hagedoorn, Jean-François Hennart, and Ted Kumpe for reading the book and providing me with their critical remarks. Brigitte Brech, Alex. Schröder, Rob Steenhorst, and Esther Verduin assisted me very well during the data collection and data processing. A pleasant working environment is and has been important to me. I want to thank all my present and former colleagues of the Organization and Strategy Section at Tilburg University for creating this ideal situation. I am very grateful to Aswin van Oijen for letting me use his database of Dutch firms.

I would like to thank Ruud Frambach, Patrick Leunissen, Bertrand Melenberg, and Rik Pieters for their willingness to answer my methodological questions, Nancy Kanters for the dedication with which she perfected the lay-out, and Hildegard Penn for correcting my English. I appreciate the cooperation of all respondents very much.

A last expression of gratitude is directed at all the people in my immediate environment. I know that you all must have suffered from my efforts to write this book.

John Bell

1 Introduction

Internationalization is an important issue on the strategic agenda of firms. When the home market is too small or competition is too strong for firms to be profitable, firms are forced to seek new possibilities either of increasing benefits or of decreasing the costs of production. A reduction in costs can, for instance, be achieved by moving production facilities to low-wage countries, while sales can be increased by entering new geographical markets. In the last few decades, opportunities for entering new markets have improved considerably. Many countries have opened their markets to foreign investors, new markets have emerged, customer preferences across the world have converged, and the developments in information technology have facilitated the management of foreign affiliates.

However, each foreign entry remains difficult, mainly because of the many factors that affect the success of the entry. Firms that want to invest in a foreign country should assess the possible impact of these factors. Despite the complexity of this decision-making process, it is important that firms make the right decision within the right span of time. Generally, firms have only one real chance to enter a foreign market (Hill, Hwang, and Kim, 1990; Root, 1987; Terpstra and Sarathy, 1991; Wind and Perlmutter, 1977). If the first attempt fails, other firms may profit from the opportunities, which makes a second attempt futile. In addition, foreign entry usually requires substantial investments, which will be worthless when the entry fails.

The purpose of the present study is to provide insight into the factors that are decisive for the foreign entry mode choice. Rather than attempting to cover the whole range of possible modes of entry, the focus will be on the question whether a firm should enter a foreign market on its own, with a single venture or a wholly owned subsidiary (WOS), or together with a partner firm in a joint venture (JV) (see, e.g., Agarwal,

1994; Agarwal and Ramaswami, 1992a, 1992b; Benito, 1996; Erramilli, 1991; Erramilli and Rao, 1993; Gatignon and Anderson, 1988; Gomes-Casseres, 1989; Hennart, 1991; Kim and Hwang, 1992; Kogut and Singh, 1988b; Larimo, 1993; Padmanabhan and Cho, 1994). In this study, a WOS is defined as a fully controlled affiliate, set up from scratch.[1] A JV is defined as a cooperative relationship between at least two firms which contribute resources to a newly formed joint subsidiary in exchange for shares in the control over and the equity of the new entity.

The main reason for investigating only these two types is that the two modes are comparable: both involve the development of new activities from scratch. In a WOS, however, the investing firm can build upon its own skills and experiences only, whereas a JV enables the combination and integration of the partners' capabilities. Particularly if the partners' skills and experiences are complementary, synergetic advantages may be gained in a JV. This shared characteristic distinguishes WOSs and JVs from full and partial acquisitions which can utilize existing facilities. A comparison between start-ups and acquisitions would lead to a different research question. In that case, the focus would be on the question whether to create an affiliate from scratch or to build upon existing facilities. This choice was the topic of several empirical studies (see, e.g., Caves and Mehra, 1986; Cho and Padmanabhan, 1995; Hennart and Park, 1993; Kogut and Singh, 1988a; Wilson, 1980; Zejan, 1990), but will not be considered in this study.

A second common feature of WOSs and JVs is that the relationship with the new subsidiary is not only a contractual one, but also involves participation in its equity. This distinguishes WOSs and JVs from non-equity modes of foreign entry, such as exporting and licensing. Studies that examined, for instance, the choice between WOSs and licensing arrangements concentrated on the expanding firm's eagerness to own the foreign venture or not. A number of studies investigated this decision (see, e.g., Bilkey and Tesar, 1977; Contractor, 1984; Davidson and McFetridge, 1985; Killing, 1980; Shane, 1994; Tallman, 1991).

Several studies have explored the factors that influence the choice between JVs and WOSs (Agarwal and Ramaswami, 1992a, 1992b; Benito, 1996; Erramilli, 1991; Erramilli and Rao, 1993; Gatignon and Anderson, 1988; Gomes-Casseres, 1989, 1990; Hennart, 1991; Kim and Hwang, 1992; Larimo, 1993). These studies revealed a large number of variables which appear to be relevant predictors for the incidence of JVs or WOSs.

Some studies used transaction cost economics (see, e.g., Williamson, 1975, 1985) as a framework for formulating hypotheses (e.g., Agarwal,

1994; Agarwal and Ramaswami, 1992b; Davidson and McFetridge, 1985; Erramilli, 1991; Erramilli and Rao, 1993; Gatignon and Anderson, 1988; Hennart, 1991). This theoretical framework is oriented towards selecting the most efficient governance structures. It is a useful framework for entry mode choices, but, as is increasingly being acknowledged, this theory can provide only a partial explanation of the complex, multi-faceted foreign entry mode decision-making process. Therefore, researchers have attempted to incorporate concepts of other theories into the frameworks of their studies (Agarwal and Ramaswami, 1992a; Bell, 1993a; Gomes-Casseres, 1989, 1990; Hennart and Park, 1993; Hill, Hwang, and Kim, 1990; Madhok, forthcoming). These attempts show that a combination of more than one perspective can be fruitful. The most elaborate framework is the eclectic theory of the foreign entry mode choice as introduced by Hill, Hwang, and Kim (1990). They integrated aspects of three theories (transaction cost economics, internalization theory, and strategic behaviour approach) into one eclectic model.[2] This eclectic framework, however, is not specified very precisely, and some potentially relevant variables are ignored. The present study builds on this eclectic theory. Several extensions and adjustments will be made based on a critical review of the international business literature, strategic management literature, and previous empirical studies on foreign entry mode choices. Hence, this study will present a new eclectic, and more comprehensive, conceptual framework for examining the selection of foreign entry modes.

Most previous empirical studies assumed that the relevant factors for the foreign entry mode choice could be adequately captured with archival data. In doing so, researchers disregard the crucial role of the perception of decision makers. Irrespective of the actual circumstances, decision makers take decisions that are based on their own judgment of the situation. Ignoring the decisive influence of perception is a weakness in most entry mode studies. Only recently, some researchers acknowledged the importance of incorporating perceptions. They used surveys instead of publicly available sources to collect data on foreign entry mode decisions (Agarwal and Ramaswami, 1992a; Erramilli, 1991; Kim and Hwang, 1992; Larimo, 1993; Madhok, 1994). The present study also recognizes the relevance of perceptions. Therefore, a survey was conducted to obtain data on foreign entry mode decisions. These subjective data were complemented with archival data. This combination of data adds to previous studies that only used either subjective or objective data.

Closely related to this issue is the measurement of the explanatory variables. Nearly all previous studies used one-item proxies for the variables, usually gathered at an aggregated level (e.g., the industry level). However, many variables are complex constructs which cannot be assessed using one single indicator. Hence, multiple proxies at the firm or venture level should be employed to improve the measurement of such complex variables. In line with Agarwal and Ramaswami (1992a), Kim and Hwang (1992), and Madhok (1994), the present study will combine multiple indicators (at the level of the venture or the firm) to measure explanatory variables.

Finally, most studies are based on entries of US MNEs (e.g., Agarwal and Ramaswami, 1992a, 1992b; Brouthers et al., 1993; Caves and Mehra, 1986; Contractor, 1984; Davidson and McFetridge, 1985; Erramilli, 1991; Erramilli and Rao, 1993; Gatignon and Anderson, 1988; Gomes-Casseres, 1989, 1990; Kim and Hwang, 1992). This bias concerning the national background of the firms examined (i.e., country-of-origin effects) may have had its repercussions on the external validity of the results. The number of studies that investigated foreign entry decisions of European firms is rather limited (see, e.g., Barkema, Bell, and Pennings, 1996; Benito, 1996; Larimo, 1993). The same can be observed for the number of Japanese entry studies (see, e.g., Cho and Padmanabhan, 1995; Hennart, 1991; Hennart and Park, 1993; Hennart and Reddy, 1992; Padmanabhan and Cho, 1994). The present study focuses on expansions of Dutch MNEs to find out whether the results of studies on US-based firms are valid in other countries. In this regard, this study, which is the first large-scale cross-sectional study on foreign entries of Dutch MNEs, responds to the call for more research on foreign entries of non-US firms (see Brouthers et al., 1993).

In sum, the present study adds to previous studies in several respects. First, a more comprehensive, eclectic framework will be developed. Second, this framework will be tested using data from foreign entries of Dutch MNEs. Third, these data include the perceptions of decision makers as well as archival data. Fourth, the data involve data on the level of the firm and of the foreign affiliate. Fifth, multiple indicators are utilized to measure complex explanatory constructs.

1.1 Problem formulation

The central issue of this study concerns the comparison between JVs and WOSs as alternative modes of foreign entry. More specifically, an attempt will be made to determine the variables that affect the choice between the two entry modes.

Formally, the main research question is:

What factors influence the choice between a joint venture (JV) and a greenfield wholly owned subsidiary (WOS) as the mode of foreign entry?

1.2 Structure of the book

In Chapter 2, the strategic relevance of foreign entry mode selections is indicated, and the definitions of a number of possible modes of foreign entry are given. Next, a critical overview of theories on international business is provided. Finally, an overview is presented of previous empirical studies on the choice between JV and WOS.

In Chapter 3, the conceptual framework is developed. This eclectic framework serves as the basis for the formulation of the hypotheses.

In Chapter 4, the methods of data collection and the measurement of the variables are described. Furthermore, an outline is given of the statistical techniques that are used to process the data in two successive steps: creating the measurement model and testing the hypotheses.

In Chapter 5, the results of the two-step analysis are discussed. First, the results of the estimations of the constructs are presented, and afterwards the findings of the hypotheses testing.

Chapter 6 contains the conclusions of the present study and some managerial implications. Finally, some suggestions for further research are provided.

Notes

1 The abbreviation WOS is only used for wholly owned greenfield investments or wholly owned start-ups. Acquisitions that lead to full control are not included in the term WOS.
2 The authors do not report explicitly that these three theoretical approaches are combined in their eclectic framework. They only speak of strategic variables, environmental variables, and transaction variables. However, as will be demonstrated in the present study, these three groups of variables are closely related to the theories mentioned.

2 Literature review

This chapter provides a review of the literature on entry mode choice. However, before presenting the state of the art, the entry mode choice will first be placed in a broader perspective. In section 2.1, the position of the entry mode choice in the firm's strategy will be considered. Next, various modes of entry will be described (section 2.2). Section 2.3 and 2.4 contain a critical review and comparison of theories on international business. In section 2.5, an overview of previous empirical research will be presented. This chapter ends with the conclusions (section 2.6).

2.1 Corporate strategy and the choice of entry mode

Most firms have two levels of strategies: corporate strategy and business unit (or competitive) strategy (Porter, 1987). Competitive strategy concerns the way in which each business unit should compete within its industry. Only by creating a distinctive competitive advantage,[1] each business unit may be able to achieve the best competitive position. Possible strategies to enhance the firm's competitive position are cost leadership, product differentiation, cost focus, differentiation focus (Porter, 1980), shelter (Rugman and Verbeke, 1990), or cooperation (Moon, 1993). Corporate strategy, in contrast, concerns the choice of the businesses a firm wants to operate in, and the management of the different business units (Porter, 1987). Corporate strategy should be the catalyst which generates synergies over and above the efforts of the separate business units. This value added can be achieved by coordinating and aligning the activities and requirements of the business units. Corporate strategy, thus, entails the survival and the continuity of the firm. Stated differently, corporate strategy deals with the question: 'How should a firm manage its growth and development to maximize long-run profitability?' (Hill and Jones, 1989). The answer to this question requires that the businesses *and* the markets the firm wants to compete in are known. Corporate strategy determines whether the firm will concentrate on a single business, will integrate vertically into other stages of the value chain, or will diversify into other businesses (Ansoff, 1965; Hill and Jones, 1989). These businesses may be located either in the home country or in other countries.

In the last decades, many firms have established a presence in foreign markets (Bartlett and Ghoshal, 1989; Levitt, 1983; Ohmae, 1985). In fact, a shift from product-market expansion to geographic market expansion can be observed (Dunning, 1993). Internationalization of activities is becoming a prerequisite for the continuity of many firms, and should not be ignored in the process of strategy formation.

The process of strategy formation involves many decisions. It includes the selection of product-market combinations, the decision to enter a foreign market or to stay within national borders (see, e.g., Aharoni, 1966), the choice of target countries, and the determination of the firm's competitive strategy in the various product-market combinations. All separate decisions in this process of strategy formation interact with one another and are, thus, very important. Together they determine the firm's competitiveness. Consequently, a thorough ex-ante deliberation of the relationships between the various decisions is required. All decisions must be geared to one another. Therefore, it would be inappropriate to devote most attention to only one decision in the entire process of strategy formation, thereby ignoring the other decisions.

A good example of such a narrow focus on only one decision is Porter's (1980) approach. In his book, Porter concentrated on the final decision of the strategy process, i.e., competitive positioning. He argued that firms should choose one of three generic strategies (cost leadership, differentiation, or focus) to strengthen their competitive position. Porter suggested that this selection from among the three generics is the most important decision to be made. The determination of the precise criteria for selection takes place in isolation from the other decisions. As a result, a possible interdependence of this final decision in the process of strategy formation on previous decisions remains uncovered. Although the choice of competitive strategy is essential, a 'correct' generic strategy will not lead to the best attainable competitive position if earlier decisions are suboptimal. Porter's generic strategies may be compared to the choices to be made in the last kilometre of a marathon, while it may be more useful to investigate what choices are made in the first 41 kilometres (Rugman and Verbeke, 1993a, p. XI).

More recently, Porter (1986) acknowledged the relevance of other important decisions in the process of strategy formation, such as the configuration and coordination of foreign activities (see also Bartlett and Ghoshal, 1989). The configuration of the firm's activities includes how many subsidiaries are established, and where (i.e., the location) they are established. Coordination involves the structuring of the relationship between headquarters and the various separate entities (Porter, 1986). Although this distinction and interpretation of the two concepts are susceptible to criticism, the relevance of the configuration and coordination of foreign activities in the process of strategy formation is generally accepted. Some of the criticism is put forward by Rugman and Verbeke (1993b), who argued that both concepts are too broad to be useful as criteria when choosing among alternatives. Further, they claimed that the concepts of configuration and coordination are not mutually exclusive (see also Moon, 1992).

One very important issue of international configuration, and consequently also an essential element in the process of strategy formation, is the choice of the mode of entry (Anderson and Gatignon, 1986; Hill, Hwang, and Kim, 1990; Kogut and Singh, 1988a; Root, 1987; Terpstra and Sarathy, 1991; Wind and Perlmutter, 1977) or of the package of different entry modes (Benito and Welch, 1994).[2] After choosing in what product-market combinations and where a firm wants to operate, the mode of entry must be determined. MNEs can choose among many entry modes when entering a new product or geographical market. This choice has major consequences for other decisions in the process of strategy formation and should, therefore, be considered very carefully. A firm may gain significant advantages *vis-à-vis* competitors when the correct entry mode is selected. For example, if the environment requires a fast entry to ensure a large market share, a WOS will not be the most appropriate mode of entry. Then, other modes with a shorter set-up time are to be preferred.

Furthermore, firms have to select the right mode of entry the first time. Often, there are no possibilities for a second chance (Davidson, 1982; Root, 1987). Whenever a second-best entry mode is chosen, (potential) competitors may already have taken the opportunities to serve the product-market combination. In addition to the market potential lost, many committed resources (e.g., management time, money, and various facilities) may become obsolete. These far-reaching consequences of an incorrect choice show that the mode of foreign entry should be selected correctly the first time. There is no general rule which states when a specific mode of entry is the most appropriate alternative, since all entry modes have unique characteristics. In the following chapters, the contingencies for the optimal mode of entry will be elaborated. In the next section, an overview will be given of the various possible modes of foreign entry.

2.2 Possible modes of entry

There are many possible modes of entry. The modes which are relevant to foreign market entry are discussed in this section. Since JVs and WOSs have been described in Chapter 1, they will be left out of the following overview.

The first mode of foreign entry that will be described is *exporting*. Exporting can take place in different ways. For instance, products can be sold in other countries via arm's-length contracts. This means that only one transaction takes place without the intention of establishing a relationship.[3] Another way of exporting is using a local agent. A third option is to establish a sales office, which sells the products of the exporting firm.

Countertrade is a collection of entry modes which have in common that the seller has a contractual obligation to purchase products back from the buyer (Banks, 1983). Countertrade comprises no less than about 5 per cent of total world trade (OECD, 1985). Many researchers have pointed to the increasing relevance of countertrade as the number of firms and countries involved in countertrade had been growing in the 1980s (Carter and Gagne, 1988; Choudry, McGeady, and Stiff, 1989; Francis, 1987; Hennart, 1990). However, a substantial part of the countertrade value consisted of trade with the former centrally planned economies (Hennart, 1990). After Eastern European countries opened up their markets to other modes of entry, countertrade lost some of its attractiveness.

Following Hennart (1990), six forms of countertrade can be distinguished, which are divided into two groups. The common characteristic of the first three types of countertrade (barter, clearing arrangements, and switch trading) is that cash payments are avoided.[4] *Barter* is the most primitive form of trade whereby products are exchanged, just like in ancient times. *Clearing arrangements* are compilations of large numbers of barters in order to create the possibility of credit. Surpluses or shortages are periodically settled in cash or in kind (Halbach and Osterkamp, 1989). In the case of *switch trading*, the positions which are kept in clearing arrangements can be traded, thus enhancing the flexibility of the arrangements (Hennart, 1990).

The other three forms of countertrade (buy back, counterpurchase, and offset) have in common that the parties involved enter into mutual obligations, laid down in parallel contracts (Halbach and Osterkamp, 1989; Hennart, 1990). In a *buy-back* arrangement, technological know-how and assistance are transferred to another country in exchange for money. A parallel agreement contains detailed arrangements about the amount of products which are made with the knowledge provided that will be bought by the seller of the technology. *Counterpurchases* differ from buy backs in the sense that there is no connection between the technologies sold and the products bought. The last form of countertrade is *offset*, which deals with the compensation a host country gets for the payments it has made for the technologies delivered. In an offset, the exporting firm does not only have to buy products from the host country, but may also be obliged to outsource part(s) of its production process to local firms or to transfer more technologies to the host country. This type of countertrade is very common in the military defence industry (Hennart, 1990).

A *cartel* is an entry mode which is subjected to stringent legislation. It is a temporary form of horizontal cooperation in which economically independent participants make verbal or written agreements to change the market conditions in their favour, often by means of market control (Hoekman, 1984; De Jong, 1985). Most cartels are prohibited by anti-cartel laws, as they cause unfair competition. A well-known example of a cartel is the OPEC, which attempts to make agreements on the quantity of the barrels of oil to be produced and on its prices.

Licensing agreements are long-term contracts which cover the transfer of the right to use specific know-how. Generally, the licensee pays the licensor a royalty based on the quantity or the sales of the output which embodies the know-how transferred. Sometimes, however, (packages of) patents are exchanged for other patents making actual payment unnecessary. This type of agreement is labelled a cross-licensing arrangement. The knowledge transferred may concern one or more products, the production process, or the R&D activities representing current technologies or current *and* future technologies (Killing, 1980). In the latter case, new developments in a specified product range will be transferred to the licensee too. In order to make the know-how transferable, it should be recorded in a blueprint, a drawing, or a formula. When the know-how is of a tacit nature (Polanyi, 1967), it cannot be transferred in the form of a written contract. Tacit knowledge can only be acquired via learning-by-doing, which is usually not incorporated in the licensing agreement. Sometimes, however, a minor part of the arrangement involves the teaching of certain specific activities. For example, when a brewery licenses its knowledge to brew beer to a foreign firm, it will also provide training facilities to assure the quality of the beer and its brewing process. Although the precise process can be described in a formula or a blueprint, a 'Fingerspitzengefühl' or 'gut feeling' is required for the way to react to unforeseeable events, and the finishing touch. This feeling can only be obtained by experience.

Licenses are becoming more and more popular vehicles for the transfer of the newest technologies to competitors. The main underlying argument for this rather paradoxical tendency[5] is that firms attempt to create a global standard for technological innovations. Philips, for instance, has licensed its technological know-how of the production of compact discs and players to several competitors, including Sony. Philips's intention was to prevent a debacle similar to what happened with the introduction of the Video 2000 system some years earlier. A global standard at an early stage of development enables firms to be profitable without the threat of intensive competition.

Franchising is also called commercial licensing (Hoekman, 1984). It can be described as a contractual form of commercial cooperation between independent firms, where the franchisee pays for the right to use the franchiser's brand name and, possibly, other distinctive means, such as the lay-out and the design of the shop (Brickley and Dark, 1987). Both firms remain independent. Popular examples of firms using franchising as a mode of foreign entry are McDonalds, Burger King, and Pizza Hut.

Another contractual mode of entry is the *consortium*, which is frequently confused with a JV. The main difference is that, in contrast with JVs, no equity participation takes place. A consortium is a sort of contractual JV, which is set up for the duration of a project. A number of firms establish a relationship to share the expenses and the risk of a (large) project. Examples of projects that typically require a consortium are the exploration of oilfields, the construction of huge buildings, and the construction of the Channel Tunnel.

Another possible mode of entry is a *strategic alliance*, an umbrella term used for many forms of cooperation. A large variety of coalitions, such as JVs, marketing agreements, supply agreements, licensing agreements and so forth, are labelled strategic alliances (see, e.g., Harrigan, 1988b; Porter and Fuller, 1986). Most definitions of strategic alliances are very broad, for instance: partnerships among firms that work together to attain some strategic objective (Berg, Duncan, and Friedman, 1982; Killing, 1983). A better definition of a strategic alliance is the one formulated by Burgers, Hill, and Kim (1993), who state that a strategic alliance is a long-term explicit contractual agreement pertaining to an exchange and/or combination of some, but not all, of a firm's resources with a competitor. This definition does not include JVs, since no reference is made to equity participation, which is a distinctive feature of JVs.

A *minority participation* involves the purchase of a small percentage of the equity of an ongoing firm, usually a small high-tech firm (Harrigan, 1986). Often, such an investment is focused on keeping up with and, eventually, acquiring the specific skills or know-how of the target firm. One of the characteristics of minority participations as opposed to JVs or acquisitions is that the specific nature and identity of the target firm are preserved. It helps to avoid that the innovative capabilities and the flexibility of the small firm are influenced by the negative impact of a larger firm's bureaucratic, time-consuming decision-making processes. Minority participations may be used as a sort of venture capital to provide entrepreneurs with the capital required.

The last entry mode to be considered here is the *acquisition*. This is the most far-reaching mode of entry, as all resources of a target firm are absorbed by the buying firm. This feature typically distinguishes an acquisition from a JV, where only a part of a firm's resources is exchanged.[6] In the terms of Williamson (1975, 1985), acquisitions are regarded as hierarchical governance structures as the buying firm obtains full ownership and, consequently, full control of the target firm. The acquired firm must be integrated into the buying firm to increase the likelihood that the acquisition will be successful (Bueno and Bowditsch, 1989). This process of integration is often subject to many problems and misunderstandings, which are usually due to differences between the partners' corporate culture. If a foreign firm is acquired, the combination and integration of the firms are much more complex than if a firm is acquired with the same home base. In the former case, both national and corporate cultural differences have to be overcome. Acquisitions may be used to obtain market power by creating an oligopolistic or even a monopolistic market situation. Anti-trust legislation, however, attempts to prevent the creation of market power and may, therefore, prohibit certain acquisitions.

In the next section, a selection of relevant theories on internationalization will be discussed.

2.3 Theories on international business

The internationalization of firms is a topic which has been studied from many different disciplines, like international finance, international trade, and international business. The present study focuses on international business, in which several explanations of the internationalization of firms can be distinguished. This suggests that there is a lack of consensus about the conceptual domain of international business (Toyne, 1989). These approaches can be divided into two broad groups: static and dynamic approaches.

Static approaches compare different states instead of processes, and try to find the best solution (e.g., the best ownership structure) for a certain state. They provide explanations for the existence of MNEs, and not for the process of internationalization (Melin, 1992). Most of these static approaches have an economic background, which means that they evaluate firms' involvements in foreign countries based on their costs and benefits. Examples of static approaches are: Hymer's theory (Hymer, 1960, 1976), transaction cost economics (Hennart, 1982; Teece, 1981, 1986; Williamson, 1975, 1985), internalization theory (Buckley and Casson, 1976; Rugman, 1981), Dunning's eclectic paradigm (Dunning, 1981, 1988a, 1988b), the strategic behaviour approach (Kogut, 1988), the resource-based approach (Wernerfelt, 1984), and the eclectic theory of the choice of the international entry mode (Hill, Hwang, and Kim, 1990).

Dynamic approaches, in contrast, consider internationalization to be a sequential process. They attempt to explain and predict the firm's involvement in the international environment over time. Examples of dynamic models are: the product life-cycle model (Vernon, 1966, 1979), the innovation-adoption-inspired internationalization models (Andersen, 1993; Bilkey and Tesar, 1977; Cavusgil, 1980), and the Uppsala internationalization process model (Johanson and Vahlne, 1977, 1990; Johanson and Wiedersheim-Paul, 1975; Welch and Luostarinen, 1988).

Given the aim of this study (see Chapter 1), namely to investigate what factors underlie the choice for a JV or a WOS in foreign-entry decisions, static approaches are more appropriate than dynamic ones. Hence, this study will only concentrate on static approaches. It should be stressed, however, that the focus will be on theories which provide microlevel (i.e., firm-level) explanations for the existence of MNEs. More macroeconomic and financial theories on the MNE (e.g., Aliber, 1970; Kojima, 1978, 1982; Kojima and Ozawa, 1984; Lessard, 1976, 1982; Rugman, 1975, 1979) are disregarded in this study.[7]

First, a description will be given of static theoretical concepts that provide an answer to the question why firms become MNEs. Next, these theoretical concepts will be evaluated in section 2.4. Finally, previous empirical studies will be reviewed (section 2.5).

Hymer's market imperfections theory of foreign direct investment

Hymer (1960) was the first to explain foreign direct investment (FDI) as an international extension of industrial organization theory. He criticized the model of perfect competition of neoclassical economics, which asserts that international trade is the only possible way to have international involvement (Kindleberger, 1969). In his pioneering dissertation, Hymer (1960, 1976) challenges the assumption of the model of perfect competition that information is costless and freely available. According to Hymer, local firms are better informed about the local economic situation than foreign firms. In order to be able to provide an explanation for the existence of FDI, two conditions must be fulfilled: (1) MNEs that own and control foreign subsidiaries must possess firm-specific advantages that outweigh the disadvantages of being a foreign firm, and (2) the market for selling these advantages must be imperfect (Hymer, 1960, 1976). These firm-specific advantages, which Hymer called monopolistic advantages (based on market power), imply the existence of structural market imperfections. Hymer relied on Bain (1956) in rationalizing these imperfections, such as knowledge advantages, distribution networks, economies of scale, and product differentiation. Hymer's view on MNEs as monopolistic rent seekers formed the basis for Kindleberger's (1969) 'market imperfections paradigm' and for Caves's (1971) early work. Hymer's market imperfections theory of FDI postulates that WOSs are the best alternative in the case of monopolistic advantages, while arm's-length transactions are the best alternative in the absence of these advantages.

Hymer (1960, 1976) emphasized the role of monopoly power in explaining MNEs, and paid no attention to efficiency based or Coasian (Coase, 1937) considerations (Dunning, 1988a, 1988b; Dunning and Rugman, 1985; Rugman, 1986; Teece, 1985, 1986). Obviously, Hymer was not aware of Coase's work when completing his dissertation in 1960 (Horaguchi and Toyne, 1990). However, in his later work (Hymer, 1968, 1970), he explicitly referred to Coase and even combined Coase's view of markets and firms with his own market imperfection theory of MNEs. For example, Hymer (1968) concluded that the international activities of firms are determined by both market power and cost considerations.

Transaction cost economics

Oliver Williamson (1975, 1985) uses the concept of transaction cost market imperfections in his analytical framework. He builds on Coase

(1937), who rationalized the existence of firms and specified the conditions of market failure. Transaction cost economics elaborates Coase's views focusing on the most efficient governance structure for a given type of transaction. Hence, the level of analysis in transaction cost economics is the transaction. A transaction is defined as 'the transfer of a good or service across a technologically separable interface' (Williamson, 1975, 1985). A 'most efficient' governance structure means that the total production and transaction costs are, in the long run, less than those of any other governance structure. Production costs include the direct and indirect costs of making the products, such as the costs of labour, energy, raw materials, semi-manufactured products, components, depreciation of the machinery, and maintenance. Transaction costs are the costs connected with finding a contractual partner, specifying a contract, and securing that the ex-ante defined goals will be met ex post (Williamson, 1975, 1985). These transaction costs are determined by three characteristics of transactions (asset specificity, uncertainty/complexity, and frequency), given two assumptions about human behaviour (bounded rationality and opportunism) (Williamson, 1975).

Different combinations of the three characteristics of transactions will lead to different optimal governance structures. Firms prefer to internalize transactions (i.e., creating a WOS or, in Williamsonian language, a hierarchy) in cases of highly specific assets, high uncertainty, and recurrent transactions. This governance structure is the best safeguard against opportunistic behaviour. In a hierarchy, authority and rules can be used to ensure that employees will not behave in an opportunistic way (Williamson, 1975, 1985).

JVs, however, can only exist if the markets for intermediate inputs are inefficient (Hennart, 1988). Then, JVs will be the most efficient governance structure when transactions are characterized by a moderate level of asset specificity, uncertainty, and frequency. Given these transaction cost market imperfections, JVs are the best alternative for coordinating assets which can be shared at zero or low marginal cost (i.e., public goods), and cannot be separated from unwanted assets (i.e., firm-specific assets) (Hennart, 1988). In order to remain the most efficient alternative, it is important that effective safeguards exist against the risk of opportunistic behaviour of the partner(s). Several researchers proposed solutions for ensuring effective safeguards. For instance, Buckley and Casson (1988) introduced a theory of cooperation in which the concepts of mutual forbearance, mutual commitment, and mutual trust (see also Beamish and Banks, 1987) are crucial. Mutual forbearance means that all partners claim that they will refrain from cheating. Important in this respect is that the commitment to the relationship is credible to all partners. From this perspective, cooperation is efficient if a given amount of mutual forbearance generates the largest possible amount of mutual trust. In a similar vein, Kogut (1988) distinguished two critical issues, namely the rules concerning the division of control and the sharing of gains and/or losses, and the mutual commitment of resources. Brown, Rugman, and Verbeke (1989) emphasized, in this regard, that the reward and control system should reflect each partner's contribution to the JV correctly.

Initially, transaction cost economics focused on explaining why and when a particular governance structure is chosen, neglecting the international context. Williamson (1992) admits that his analysis of MNEs is brief and incomplete. Notwithstanding this observation, it should be stressed that this rather unexplored field was developed by others than Williamson (see Anderson and Gatignon, 1986; Buckley and Casson, 1985; Casson, 1982; Caves, 1982; Hennart, 1982; Klein, Frazier, and Roth, 1990; Teece, 1981, 1986). For instance, Teece (1986) asserted that MNEs prefer to internalize certain transactions to reduce the effects of opportunistic behaviour, which can be very great in an international environment.

Internalization theory

Internalization theory was developed to provide an economic rationale for the existence of MNEs (Buckley and Casson, 1976; McManus, 1972).[8] The firm is the unit of analysis. This theory rests on two general axioms (Buckley, 1988): (1) firms choose the least cost location for each activity they perform, and (2) firms grow by internalizing markets up to the point where the benefits of further internalization are outweighed by the costs. The first axiom did not always receive the attention it deserved. Rugman (1981), for instance, minimized the relevance of location-specific variables (e.g., low labour costs, low transport costs, and a good infrastructure) in internalization theory by including spatial cost saving as a firm-specific variable. He argued that the location-specific variables are exogenous and only have an explanatory value at the macrolevel, not at the level of the individual firm. Buckley (1983) criticized this point of view by referring to the vital role the location choice and the non-traded inputs play in the competitive positioning and growth pattern of firms.

Rugman and Verbeke (1992, 1993b) proposed a modified internalization theory, which is based on concepts from authors who combined the field of strategic management with international business (e.g., Bartlett and Ghoshal, 1989; Doz, 1986; Ghoshal, 1987). Rugman and Verbeke made an explicit distinction between firm-specific advantages and country-specific advantages, whereby the former can be either location bound or non-location bound. Location-bound firm-specific advantages will only yield benefits in a particular environment. An exchange or diffusion of the location-bound advantages to other locations is no option, as it will make the advantages worthless. The non-location-bound advantages, however, keep their value when transferred to and applied in additional locations. This distinction of two types of firm-specific advantages clearly shows the importance of locational differences.

In its most general sense, the second axiom can be interpreted as being tautological, or as Buckley (1983) formulated it eloquently: 'a concept in search of a theory'. However, additional assumptions about transaction costs for particular products and for trade between particular locations were specified (Casson, 1982). For example, the market for know-how is imperfect, long-term contracts are difficult to specify and to enforce, and tariffs and other financial burdens cause internal transfer pricing. The firm is an alternative to a market, as the internal market is used to produce and distribute goods and services efficiently in cases of (external) market failures (Rugman, 1982). MNEs arise when markets across national borders are internalized. Markets that are often internalized are intermediate markets with imperfections, such as markets for knowledge (Buckley and Casson, 1976; Hennart, 1982; Rugman, 1981). MNEs possess a comparative advantage when transactions are uncertain and when transactions consist of long-term exchanges of complex and heterogeneous products among a relatively small number of traders.

According to the original internalization theory, MNEs always avoid JVs since they are inferior to WOSs, which allow MNEs to maximize the returns on ownership-specific advantages (Caves, 1982). JVs and other hybrid forms of coordination are fraught with danger for the MNE, as they may negatively affect the MNE's firm-specific advantage (Rugman, 1982). The benefits of cooperation could never offset the strategic risks and transaction costs. Referring to a study by Buckley and Davies (1981), Rugman (1982) claims that hybrid forms of coordination (including JVs and licensing) are not very important, and are unlikely to increase in number substantially in the future. They are only expected to arise when the risk of dissipation of the MNE's firm-specific advantage is low, which may be valid for only a few products (Rugman, 1982). Internalization theory, thus, cannot explain JVs (Dunning, 1989; Parry, 1985). Beamish and Banks (1987), however, extended internalization theory by providing an economic rationale for JVs. Using the transaction cost framework, Beamish and Banks (1987) argued that in situations where a JV is established in a spirit of mutual trust and commitment to its long-term success, problems regarding uncertainty, opportunism, and small numbers can be effectively dealt with. Then, the benefits of a JV will more than offset the costs.

Dunning's eclectic paradigm

The eclectic paradigm (Dunning, 1981, 1988a, 1989, 1993) recognizes that both structural and transaction cost market imperfections are important in explaining MNEs. The unit of analysis is the (whole) population of firms engaged in foreign value-adding activities. The eclectic paradigm of international production states that firms will become MNEs if three conditions are satisfied simultaneously: firms have ownership-specific advantages, which can be more profitably exploited outside the firm's domestic markets (location-specific advantage), and internalization of these advantages obtains the highest value (Dunning, 1981; Teece, 1986).[9]

Dunning (1981) identified three types of ownership-specific advantages (O):
1   those that stem from the exclusive possession of, or access to, particular income-generating assets;
2   those that are normally enjoyed by a branch plant compared to a *de novo* firm;
3   those that are a result of geographical diversification or multinationality *per se*.

In his later work, Dunning (1988a, 1988b, 1993) made a distinction between ownership-specific *asset* advantages (Oa) and ditto *transaction* advantages (Ot). Oa corresponds with the type of ownership-specific advantages as mentioned under 1, and Ot with the other two ownership-specific advantages. The Oa advantages involve the ownership of specific assets by MNEs which other firms do not own. These assets may be either tangible, such as natural endowments and (human) capital, or intangible, such as technological know-how, managerial and marketing skills, and access to intermediate and final goods markets (Dunning, 1988a, 1993). Given the notion (Dunning, 1988b) that the differences between firms' assets can only occur in a situation of structural market imperfections,[10] the Oa advantages are similar to Hymer's monopolistic advantages (Hymer, 1960, 1976). Although Dunning (1993) asserts that the O advantages embrace Porter's competitive advantages (see, e.g., Porter, 1980, 1985), he prefers his own nomenclature in calling these O advantages monopolistic rather than competitive.

The Ot advantages include the ability of firms to capture the transactional benefits from the common governance of multiple and geographically dispersed activities (Dunning, 1988b, 1993). Some examples of these Ot advantages are the firm's experience, easy access to a variety of inputs because of the relationship with the parent company, ability to learn from cultural differences, and greater knowledge of international markets.

In addition to ownership-specific advantages, location-specific advantages (L) are essential in determining which firms will engage in cross-border value-adding activities. Although the decision of where to set up production facilities is treated separately from the other two advantages, it cannot be seen as an independent decision. These location-specific advantages include, for instance, low transport costs, the availability of resource endowments, infrastructure, economic and political stability, and low input prices.

The last strand of the OLI paradigm comprises the internalization advantages (I) that MNEs have in transferring assets within their organizations instead of via the market, because of market failures. The greater the perceived costs of transactional market failure - and the greater the benefits of circumventing market failure - the more likely it will be that MNEs exploit their ownership-specific advantages within the firm. Some possible internalization incentive advantages are high search and negotiating costs, high probability of moral hazard and adverse selection, possible lock-in situations (Buckley and Casson, 1988; Williamson, 1985), and high costs of (legal) enforcement.

Strategic behaviour approach

The strategic behaviour approach, or more generally the strategic management approach, concentrates on the way in which strategic behaviour influences the firm's competitive position (Kogut, 1988) while retaining a sufficient amount of strategic flexibility (Harrigan, 1985c). More specifically, this approach is focused on the firm's ability to compete with both existing and potential competitors (Porter, 1980). As a consequence, competitive advantages are very important in the strategic behaviour approach. Competitive advantages only last for a certain period of time (Porter, 1980), which is in contrast with monopolistic advantages that are assumed to exist eternally. This time dimension is crucial in distinguishing competitive advantages from monopolistic advantages. If a firm has a competitive advantage over other firms, it must attempt to benefit maximally from this temporary relative advantage, as competitors may catch up (Buckley, 1990).

The firm's competitive position, thus, is mainly determined by its temporary competitive advantages. This explains the rather short-term orientation of the strategic behaviour approach. Given a relative advantage, MNEs will try to maximize short-term profits, even at the expense of long-term considerations, to prevent other firms from appropriating their competitive advantage (Buckley, 1990). A WOS will be preferred over other alternative governance structures, if this serves the MNE's relative competitive position best (Contractor and Lorange, 1988b).

JVs can also function as an effective mechanism for the improvement of a firm's relative competitive position. The reasons for setting up JVs are numerous (see, e.g., Contractor and Lorange, 1988a, 1988b; Harrigan, 1985a, 1988a). MNEs are expected to establish a JV only if this mode of entry maximizes profits by improving the MNE's relative competitive position. Then, the advantages minus the disadvantages of JVs relative to all other alternative governance structures are highest (compare Contractor, 1990a). Some of the (strategic) advantages of JVs are economies of scale, learning effects, reduction of risk and competition, access to know-how, skills and assets, and so on. Disadvantages are, for instance, the cost of coordinating activities, the dissipation of know-how, and possible opportunistic behaviour (Porter and Fuller, 1986).

Resource-based theory

The resource-based view of the firm emerged only recently (see, e.g., Barney, 1986; Collis, 1991; Conner, 1991; Mahoney and Pandian, 1992; Peteraf, 1993; Tallman, 1991; Wernerfelt, 1984), although its origin can be found in the 1930s. The antecedents of the resource-based perspective originate in four different, though related, streams: the theory of imperfect competition (Chamberlin, 1933; Robinson, 1933), the theory of the growth of the firm (Penrose, 1959; Rubin, 1973), the evolutionary, entrepreneurial view of the firm (Cyert and March, 1963; Nelson and Winter, 1982; Schumpeter, 1934), and transaction cost economics (Coase, 1937; Williamson, 1975, 1985). The resource-based theory attempts to explain the success and failure of individual firms by concentrating on the heterogeneous nature of the firm-specific resources (Helleloid, 1992). A firm is considered to be a unique collection of productive resources that are heterogeneous and fungible (Penrose, 1959). The term heterogeneous means that the resources are unique, whereas fungible implies that the resources can be applied for the provision of several distinct services which yield different outputs.

A well-accepted practice in the resource-based theory is to differentiate between resources and capabilities (Amit and Schoemaker, 1993; Grant, 1991; Stalk, Evans and Shulman, 1992), also labelled tangible and intangible resources (Hall, 1992), or assets and core competencies (Prahalad and Hamel, 1990). This distinction acknowledges the difference between tangible resources (e.g., land, machines, and manufacturing facilities), which can be traded relatively easily between firms, and tacit capabilities (e.g., technological know-how, managerial know-how, financial know-how, organizational routines, and brand name capital), which are hardly transferable among firms. The firm's capabilities form the firm's capacity to use and deploy resources (Amit and Schoemaker, 1993), and infuse them with sustainable value (Madhok, forthcoming). Typical features of capabilities are that they are firm specific, difficult to imitate, and have developed over time (Amit and Schoemaker, 1993; Prahalad and Hamel, 1990). This implies that firms are able to learn from previous experiences and, in addition, can exploit the knowledge acquired in other circumstances. The accumulation of knowledge, or more generally termed capabilities, is a dynamic process which leans heavily on the history of the firm (Nelson and Winter, 1982). Current and future behaviour of firms, thus, is substantially influenced by experiences in the past. Since capabilities are the driving force behind the creation of (super-normal) rents with the firm's resources, capabilities are of the utmost importance in gaining competitive advantages. Particularly the improvement of the ability to learn (i.e., the firm's absorptive capacity; Cohen and Levinthal, 1990) by acquiring, processing, and diffusing information will result in increased advantages relative to competing firms (Ghoshal, 1987).

Firms are expected to gain (temporary) super-normal profits when they exploit their firm-specific resources efficiently and effectively to establish a good fit between strategy, structure, and environment (Helleloid, 1992; Tallman, 1991). In order to prevent the super-normal profits from being captured by competitors, firms will create resource position barriers (Wernerfelt, 1984), which will hamper the attempts to imitate the firm-specific resources. As an example, firms may decide to invest heavily in the development of technological know-how or organizational learning.

Like the other theoretical explanations in this section, the resource-based approach is able to provide a rationale for FDI. According to this theory, it is economically efficient for firms to become MNEs when the following conditions apply simultaneously (Helleloid, 1992):

1   The firm has excess capacity in a unique and valuable productive resource.
2   There are imperfect markets for these resources.
3   Exporting from the home country is less efficient than FDI because of governmental restrictions, lower factor costs, transportation

costs, and the perishability of the products.
4   Possession of unique and valuable resources gives the firm a specific advantage in the host country, which offsets the cost disadvantages of being a foreign firm.
5   The firm has the excess capacity in managerial services required to manage foreign expansion.
6   The returns from foreign expansion exceed the returns from domestic diversification.
7   The bureaucratic costs of managing one more subsidiary do not offset the potential returns.

According to the resource-based approach, the selection of the mode of foreign entry depends on the demands on the firm's capabilities and the possible increase in these capabilities (Madhok, forthcoming). Since the firm's resources and capabilities are rather constant in the short run, they both guide and restrict - in combination with the contextual requirements - the firm's entry mode choice (Tallman, 1991). An increase in the capabilities (i.e., learning) is a time-consuming, gradual process. Therefore, firms may not be able to learn the capabilities required in turbulent environments (Levitt and March, 1988). In that case, a JV is the optimal mode of entry as JVs alleviate the acquisition or development of the lacking capabilities. In addition to this reactive way of dealing with JVs, firms may also behave pro-actively or offensively by establishing JVs to increase and improve their stock of capabilities beforehand. In this regard, firms may set up JVs mainly to become experienced in managing and controlling JVs, so they can learn as much as possible from their partner's capabilities. A WOS, in contrast, is the appropriate mode of entry if the firm's current capability stock is sufficient to gain the potential rents in a foreign country.

Eclectic theory of the foreign entry mode choice

Hill, Hwang, and Kim (1990) developed a framework to combine the different and seemingly unrelated considerations and (partial) explanations discussed in the existing literature. They contended that transaction cost economics alone is not able to explain foreign entry mode choices. For example, strategic management issues, such as the role of global competition and global strategy, are completely ignored in studies using transaction cost frameworks (e.g., Gatignon and Anderson, 1988; Hennart, 1991; Hennart and Park, 1993). Therefore, Hill, Hwang, and Kim (1990) stressed the need to incorporate strategic variables in an eclectic theory of the choice of international entry modes.

They argued that the array of possible entry modes can be characterized by three constructs: the level of control, resource commitment, and the risk of dissemination. The level of control involves the amount of authority over operational and strategic decision making. Certain modes of entry provide the parent firms with more control than others. For example, in a WOS the parent firm has more influence on the decision-making processes than in a licensing arrangement. In a similar vein, it can be shown that WOSs entail more commitment of resources than JVs and licensing agreements. Lastly, the risk of dissemination refers to the risk that firm-specific advantages in know-how will be appropriated by another firm (Hill and Kim, 1988). Obviously, this risk will be much lower in the case of a WOS than in the case where less than fully controlled modes of entry are involved.

Furthermore, Hill, Hwang, and Kim (1990) distinguished three broad groups of variables that influence the entry mode decision: strategic variables, environmental variables, and transaction-specific variables. Strategic variables, being the type of strategy and the concentration in the global industry, primarily affect the entry mode decision by the level of control they require. The environmental variables (e.g., host-country risk, location familiarity, demand conditions, and the volatility of local competition) are closely connected with the commitment of resources. The final group of variables which consists of transaction-specific variables, such as the value of firm-specific know-how and the tacitness of know-how, influences the choice of the international entry mode through its impact on the risk of dissemination and the level of control.

Hill, Hwang, and Kim (1990) acknowledged that not only the separate variables are important for the choice of the foreign entry mode, but also the interaction between strategic, environmental, and transaction-specific variables. The optimal decision for the MNE is to select that entry mode that maximizes the long-term value of the firm, considering all relevant factors. WOSs are assumed to be the preferred entry mode in the case of the pursuit of a global strategy, the need for global strategic coordination, a large quasi-rent stream generated by the MNE's specific know-how, or a large tacit component of firm-specific know-how. JVs, in contrast, are expected to be preferred in the case of a multi-domestic strategy, a high country risk, a large perceived distance between the home and the host country, uncertain demand, and volatile competition in the host market.

This overview of theoretical concepts on the existence of MNEs shows that many explanations are possible. However, it appears that there is also some overlap between the explanations. In the next section, these theories will be evaluated to reveal the differences and the overlaps.

2.4 A comparative analysis of theories

In section 2.3, the following approaches were distinguished: Hymer's theory, transaction cost economics, internalization theory, Dunning's eclectic paradigm, the strategic behaviour approach, the resource-based approach, and the eclectic theory of the choice of international entry mode by Hill, Hwang, and Kim (1990). Below, these approaches will be evaluated with regard to their usefulness in explaining the choice between a JV and a WOS as the mode of foreign entry. This evaluation will be used as the basis for the construction of the conceptual framework in Chapter 3.

Hymer's market imperfections theory of FDI (Hymer, 1960, 1976) uses the concept of market power in explaining the existence of MNEs. The market power held by firms is believed to be based on monopolistic advantages of these firms. Whenever firms possess monopolistic advantages, they will invest outside their own country only by retaining full ownership (i.e., by means of WOSs). Alternatively, an arm's-length contract will be selected. This dichotomy, which Hymer proposed in his dissertation (Hymer, 1960, 1976), is a rather limited perspective as it ignores all kinds of intermediate or hybrid forms of organization, such as JVs, franchising, and licensing arrangements. A comparable narrow focus was advocated in the initial publications on transaction cost economics (Coase, 1937; Williamson, 1975). In more recent contributions, the existence of hybrid governance structures was acknowledged (Hennart, 1988; Riordan and Williamson, 1985; Williamson, 1981, 1985, 1991a, 1991b). A somewhat similar change can be observed in Hymer's work. After completing his dissertation, Hymer (1968) recognized that collusion may be an alternative to WOSs and arm's-length contracts. This can be illustrated by the following statement: 'Une firme peut s'entendre avec d'autres pour diviser le marché en sphères d'influence (par exemple, les Américains se limitant à l'Amérique Latine, les Européens à l'Asie et à l'Afrique et tous se faisant concurrence au Canada), ou bien elle peut nouer des liens de coopération plus étroits et partager avec d'autres les risques de certains entreprises .... ' (Hymer, 1968, p. 972).[11] Although Hymer acknowledged that other forms of organization are viable, he paid little attention to them. The above - rather loose - statement comes just before the end of the article, and Hymer did not elaborate on the subject in his later work.

A second point of criticism on Hymer's work is the use of monopolistic advantages, which 'automatically' lead to revenues.[12] These monopolistic advantages are firm-specific and remain valuable for a very long time without being appropriated by other firms. This conception of everlasting advantages is beyond the contemporary reality of business. Nowadays, competition is so severe that nearly every advantage a firm has over other firms will only be valuable for a short time. Competitors will try to acquire or imitate such an advantage, making the comparative advantage worthless. Even if an advantage can be patented, it will not exist forever, because the patent system is not a perfect system (Hennart, 1982). Particularly in the international context, the enforcement of patents is difficult and requires large investments of time and money (mainly for legal support). Compare, for instance, the problems firms encounter in their continuous fight against the multi-billion market of illegal imitation of a great variety of products, such as watches, compact discs, software, sportswear, and so on. Moreover, patents can fairly easily be circumvented without punishment by making a product which differs only slightly from the patented product. Hence, it can be concluded that Hymer's assumption of eternal monopolistic advantages is not realistic.

In contrast, the strategic behaviour approach and the resource-based approach explicitly acknowledge that firm-specific advantages are only temporary. Both approaches recognize that these firm-specific or competitive advantages have to be protected against the appropriation or imitation by competitors. The difference is that the resource-based approach proposes to employ resource position barriers, while the strategic behaviour approach uses entry barriers. Some examples of the former type of barriers are production experience, reputation, and relationships with clients and suppliers (Wernerfelt, 1984) or, more generally, the stock of intangible resources and skills (Dierickx and Cool, 1989). Scale economies, investments in redundant capacity, low prices, and specific non-recuperable investments (Porter, 1980) are typical examples of entry barriers.

Transaction cost economics is complementary to these two approaches, since its unit of analysis and its focus differ. Transaction cost economics evaluates decisions at the level of the individual transaction, while the strategic behaviour approach and the resource-based approach, respectively, take the firm and organizational units as the unit of analysis. Furthermore, transaction cost economics uses the long-term or structural efficiency as the criterion for choosing between alternative governance structures. The inclusion of structural efficiency considerations adds to the decision criteria of the strategic behaviour approach and, to some extent, of the resource-based approach. The strategic behaviour approach ignores the concept of structural efficiency completely, whereas the resource-based approach makes an explicit distinction between strategic intent and structural efficiency, which are integrated into one model

(Tallman, 1991). However, the attention this latter concept receives in the resource-based view is much shallower than in transaction cost economics.

In the last two decades, much criticism was addressed to transaction cost economics (see, e.g., Demsetz, 1988; Dietrich, 1994; Dow, 1993; Groenewegen, 1995; Kay, 1992; Noorderhaven, 1994; Perrow, 1986; Robins, 1987; Williamson, 1992, 1993). Some of the concepts which were criticized are the assumption of opportunism, the subordinate role of trust, the implicit assumption of hyperrationality given the explicit assumption of bounded rationality (see Noorderhaven, 1994), and so on. The focus here will be on those elements of criticism relevant for foreign entry mode choices.

Transaction cost economics only concentrates on structural efficiency at the level of the transaction, completely ignoring strategic considerations. This is especially problematic, because transaction cost economics assumes a situation of imperfect competition (Robins, 1987) in which strategic behaviour is important (see, e.g., Harrigan, 1985c; Hennart and Park, 1994; Kogut, 1988; Porter, 1980). Moreover, strategic considerations turn out to have a decisive impact on ownership decisions (Contractor, 1990a; Hennart and Park, 1994; Hill, Hwang, and Kim, 1990; Kim and Hwang, 1992; Kogut, 1988). Firms may select a mode of entry which is not efficient for the specific transaction in terms of transaction cost economics, but which is the best alternative for the firm as a whole, e.g., for strategic considerations (Kim and Hwang, 1992; Kogut, 1988; Osborn and Baughn, 1990).

A second shortcoming of transaction cost economics is that it focuses only on the minimization of costs when comparing alternative governance structures, and ignores possible benefits (Kogut, 1988). Such a one-sided approach seems to assume that the benefits are similar for all possible governance structures. However, it disregards the existence of benefits which may accrue from unique characteristics of the different modes of organization. One example is the synergy between firms which can be achieved in JVs by combining and exchanging relevant know-how. This synergy will result in higher benefits than a firm would gain in a WOS (see also Contractor, 1990a; Contractor and Lorange, 1988b). Hence, it would be more correct to consider both the benefits and the costs of governance structures when contemplating a transaction. Rather than concentrating myopically on cost minimization, a firm should attempt to maximize the difference between the benefits and the costs.

A final weakness of transaction cost economics which will be discussed here, involves the implicit assumption of identical production functions across firms (Conner, 1991; Demsetz, 1988; Dietrich, 1994; Madhok, forthcoming; Teece, 1985). This suggests that all managers of all firms have the same management capabilities and routines, and use them in the same way. This assumption is far from realistic, as it denies the existence of firm-specific differences in this area. The study by Walker and Weber (1984) supports the criticism on the above assumption, as they found that production cost differentials are more important than differences in transaction costs in make-or-buy decisions. Unlike transaction cost economics, the resource-based approach assumes that all firms have a different stock of capabilities and resources. More specifically, each firm is believed to form a unique, firm-specific bundle of resources and capabilities (Penrose, 1959).

Internalization theory, which is perceived as a general theory for the existence of the MNE (Rugman, 1979, 1981, 1985),[13] is frequently considered to be analogous to transaction cost economics. Both transaction cost economics and internalization theory rest upon the early work by Coase (1937), and were developed simultaneously in two continents. While Williamson was working on his 'markets-and-hierarchies' dichotomy, Buckley and Casson at the University of Reading (UK) formulated their internalization theory. The fundamental ideas underlying the two concepts are identical: firms use their internal organization structure to overcome problems (expressed as costs) which are caused by inefficiencies in factor markets. Both theories assume that these inefficiencies can be dealt with more efficiently within the firm than outside the firm. In this regard, Hennart (1986) stressed that organizations may fail too. As a consequence, he proposed a 'theory of firm failure', which shows that firms are not, by definition, more efficient than markets where high transaction costs are concerned. Hennart emphasized the necessity for firms to reduce shirking and to control internal loss of information. These are aspects which are more or less neglected by transaction cost economics and internalization theory.[14]

Nevertheless, there are some differences between these theories, which are merely differences in emphasis (Rugman, 1986; Teece, 1986). Transaction cost economics focuses on the level of the single transaction, whereas internalization theory takes the firm as the unit of analysis. Another difference is that the second axiom of internalization theory requires some additional constraints to prevent it from being tautological (Boddewyn, 1985; Buckley, 1983, 1988; Casson, 1982; Rugman, 1986). Only then, internalization theory is able to determine what transactions need to be internalized and what mode of entry should be selected. Transaction cost economics can provide the framework required (Teece, 1986). A last difference is that internalization theory explicitly takes location-specific advantages into account, whereas transaction cost economics disregards these advantages. Teece (1986), for example, asserts that the evaluation of location-specific advantages is nothing more than comparing, on the one hand, the unit costs of production at home and supplying the customers by exporting to, on the other hand, the costs of local production and supply. According to Teece, this is a rather straightforward conceptual exercise, which almost automatically yields the appropriate solution.

The two eclectic approaches (Dunning's eclectic paradigm and Hill, Hwang, and Kim's eclectic theory of the choice of international entry mode) also incorporate location-specific advantages. Dunning's eclectic paradigm (Dunning, 1981, 1988, 1993), which has been criticized frequently (see, e.g., Itaki, 1991; Rugman, 1986; Teece, 1986), distinguishes three kinds of advantages (OLI), which are believed to explain the foreign activities of the whole population of firms. Two of these advantages (location and internalization) are comparable with those of internalization theory, although the precise interpretation of the advantages differs. For instance, internalization theory combines ownership-specific advantages and internalization advantages since the former advantages have to be internalized to be effective (Itaki, 1991; Rugman, 1986).

Two major differences between the two eclectic frameworks are: first, Hill, Hwang, and Kim focused on the level of the individual firm, whereas Dunning attempted to explain why the whole population of MNEs developed cross-border activities. Second, Hill, Hwang, and Kim assumed that the competitive advantages of firms are temporary advantages, while Dunning's ownership-specific advantages are monopolistic advantages (compare Hymer, 1960, 1976).

A shortcoming of Hill, Hwang, and Kim's (1990) eclectic framework is that no explicit attention is paid to the resources and capabilities of firms (compare Prahalad and Hamel, 1990). Hence, the resource-based theory is not incorporated in their eclectic framework.

This section contains an evaluation of the theories. In the next chapter, the usefulness of these theories for building the conceptual framework will be examined. Before constructing that framework, a survey of previous empirical studies will be presented in the next section.

2.5 Empirical studies

Many empirical studies examined the incidence of foreign entry modes such as licensing, JVs, acquisitions, greenfield investments, franchising, exporting, and countertrade (e.g., Bilkey and Tesar, 1977; Buckley and Davies, 1981; Caves and Mehra, 1986; Contractor, 1984; Czinkota, 1982; Davidson and McFetridge, 1985; Erramilli, 1991; Gatignon and Anderson, 1988; Gomes-Casseres, 1989, 1990; Hennart, 1990, 1991; Hennart and Park, 1993; Hennart and Reddy, 1992; Kim and Hwang, 1992; Kogut and Singh, 1988a; Stopford and Wells, 1972; Welch, 1990; Wilson, 1980; Zejan, 1990). These studies tested hypotheses on a large number of variables expected to influence the choice of entry mode. Some examples are the familiarity with the host country, the cultural (dis)similarities between the firm and the host country, the degree of specificity of the assets involved, and the firm's experience with a particular entry mode, host country or industry. However, the results of these tests are mixed (see, e.g., Benito, 1996; Caves and Mehra, 1986; Contractor, 1984; Davidson and McFetridge, 1985; Gatignon and Anderson, 1988; Gomes-Casseres, 1989; Hennart, 1990, 1991; Larimo, 1993; Mariti and Smiley, 1983; Zejan, 1990). The hypotheses tested in these empirical studies were usually based on a theoretical framework as described earlier, sometimes even on more than one (Gomes-Casseres, 1989; Hennart and Park, 1993, 1994; Madhok, 1994). The frameworks most frequently used are the transaction cost framework (Agarwal and Ramaswami, 1992b; Davidson and McFetridge, 1985; Erramilli and Rao, 1993; Gatignon and Anderson, 1988; Hennart, 1991; Hennart and Reddy, 1992), the bargaining power framework (Fagre and Wells, 1982; Gomes-Casseres, 1990; Lecraw, 1984), and some eclectic frameworks (Agarwal and Ramaswami, 1992a; Kim and Hwang, 1992). Others did not use a particular framework, but elaborate on previous empirical studies (Brouthers et al., 1993; Cho and Padmanabhan, 1995; Larimo, 1993; Zejan, 1990).

As the present study focuses on the choice between JVs and WOSs, only empirical studies concerning this choice will be reviewed.[15] Table 2.1 contains an overview of the findings of these empirical studies.[16]

Stopford and Wells (1972) were the first to investigate the entry mode choice thoroughly. They analysed data on foreign entries of 155 US MNEs, and found a higher propensity to establish WOSs when marketing, product innovation, and product standardization were important. In contrast, JVs are the preferred mode of entry in extractive industries (e.g., coal mines, oil, and bauxite) and when the investment is a diversification.

Gatignon and Anderson (1988) tested eight hypotheses based on transaction cost economics (see Anderson and Gatignon, 1986)[17] regarding the level of control in establishing a foreign mode of entry. They considered the entry mode decision to be a two-stage decision. In the first stage, firms determine whether they will cooperate or not, while in the second stage the level of control (minority, 50/50, or majority) in the JV needs to be chosen. In order to test the hypotheses, Gatignon and Anderson used the database of the Harvard Multinational Enterprise Project (Curhan, Davidson and Suri, 1977). This database contains firm-level data on more than 19,000 foreign subsidiaries of the 180 largest US firms set up in the period 1900-1975. Gatignon and Anderson concentrated on the (more than 9,000) foreign entries of manufacturing firms in the period 1960-1975. However, the sample was reduced to 1,267 observations because of missing data. Their logit analyses showed that most variables have a significant impact on the decision to cooperate or not (stage 1): (a) the propensity to set up WOSs increases with the level of specific know-how, the MNE's experience, and the advertising intensity, and (b) the likelihood of JVs grows in proportion with country risk, legal restrictions, and, in certain cases, the sociocultural distance. Only three variables appeared to be significant at stage 2: a larger scale of operations leads to minority JVs; majority JVs are selected in advertising-intensive lines of business; and in Latin European countries. This study demonstrated the usefulness of a transaction cost framework for predicting the choice between a WOS and a JV. However, the small number of significant variables at stage 2 implies that this framework has insufficient predictive value for the level of control once a JV is chosen.

Kogut and Singh (1988b) particularly focused on testing the strategic behaviour approach. They distinguished the following variables: type of industry that is entered into (R&D intensive or advertising intensive), the growth of the industry entered, the degree of concentration in that industry, and the relative size of the foreign subsidiary. To investigate the impact of these strategic variables, they used the same sample as in Kogut and Singh (1988a), which was taken from a variety of publicly available sources. Their sample consisted of 108 manufacturing entries into the United States, either WOSs or JVs, made from 1981 to 1984.

Table 2.1
Overview of the findings of the empirical studies which focused on the choice between JVs and WOSs

	1	2	3	4	5	6	7	8	9	10	11	12	13	14	15	16
cultural distance	+				+			+	ns	+			+	+	-	-
physical distance									ns							
uncertainty avoidance host country												+				
power distance host country												-				
host-country risk	+						ns	-		ns				+		
level of welfare host country			+	+					-			+	-	ns		
growth of welfare host country				+					ns							
host government restrictions	+		+	+								+				
perceived market potential							-									+
resource-intensive industry			+	+		+			+							
R&D-intensive industry		+	ns	ns												
marketing-intensive intensity		ns	-	-												
industry growth		ns				+										
level of competition		ns		+		ns			ns							
market complexity											+					
desire for direct control											-					
asset specificity	-					ns	ns		ns	-				ns	ns	-
marketing intensity	-					ns										
capital intensity							-			+						
firm size				-			-		+	-				-		
size subsidiary	ns			+											ns	ns

32

	1	2	3	4	5	6	7	8	9	10	11	12	13	14	15	16
relative size	-	+				ns			ns							
international experience			-		-/+	-	-		ns					ns	-	ns
host-country experience			-	-												-
JV experience															+	
diversification			ns/+[1]	+		+			ns						ns	ns
degree of diversification			-						ns							
intra-system sales				-												
life-cycle stage									ns							
speed of internationalization									-							
export-share subsidiary									ns							
resource obsolescence															+	
contractual risk							ns									
performance ambiguity														-	ns	
service inseparability										+						

[1] Gomes-Casseres used two proxies for diversification: (1) the difference in the three-digit SIC code of the core activity of the subsidiary and the firm's activities; (2) the number of foreign subsidiaries the firm had in the subsidiary's three-digit SIC industry. Only the latter measure (i.e., product experience) was (positively) significant.

+ = increased probability of JVs; - = decreased probability of JVs; ns = not significant

1. Gatignon and Anderson (1988)
2. Kogut and Singh (1988b)
3. Gomes-Casseres (1989)
4. Gomes-Casseres (1990)
5. Erramilli (1991)
6. Hennart (1991)
7. Agarwal and Ramaswami (1992a)
8. Agarwal and Ramaswami (1992b)
9. Larimo (1993)
10. Erramilli and Rao (1993)
11. Brouthers et al. (1993)
12. Shane (1993)
13. Agarwal (1994)
14. Benito (1996)
15. Madhok (1994)
16. Padmanabhan and Cho (1994)

The results of their logit analyses partially corroborate the predictions of the strategic behaviour approach. Only two variables appear to have a significant effect on the foreign entry mode selection: the R&D intensity of the industry entered and the relative size of the investment have a positive impact on the propensity to form JVs.

Gomes-Casseres (1989) posited that the strategic motivation for cooperation, transaction costs, and organizational costs jointly determine the costs and benefits of ownership structures. In doing so, he relied explicitly on the work by Hennart (1988) and by Stopford and Wells (1972).[18] Gomes-Casseres ascertained a two-stage decision process regarding the foreign market entry mode choice, which differs from the one proposed by Anderson and Gatignon (1986). According to Gomes-Casseres, MNEs determine their own preferences with respect to the entry mode in the first stage, while in the second stage MNEs negotiate with the host government. He used the database of the Harvard Multinational Enterprise Project (Curhan, Davidson and Suri, 1977), but restricted the sample to subsidiaries which still existed in 1975. The total sample of more than 5,000 affiliates was reduced to 1,532 complete observations. With regard to the first stage, the logit models revealed that MNEs prefer JVs when they rely on local inputs of raw materials, when the host country is restrictive, and when local firms contribute skills to a JV. WOSs are preferred if MNEs have much experience in an industry or a country, when intra-system sales of the subsidiary are high, and when the subsidiary is in a marketing-intensive industry.

In an additional paper, Gomes-Casseres (1990) investigated the ownership structure of foreign entry modes in two stages: (1) What does the firm want? and (2) What can the firm get? The latter question concerns the relative bargaining power a firm has as opposed to the host government. Again, Gomes-Casseres used the Harvard Multinational Enterprise Project database, and he was able to analyse data on 1,877 foreign ventures. The results of the logit analyses are comparable with the results in Gomes-Casseres (1989): JVs are more likely in the case of host-government restrictions, if a developed country is entered, if the host country's welfare grows, in the case of a high level of competition, if a resource-intensive industry is entered, in the case of diversified expansion, and in case the subsidiary is large. In contrast, WOSs are favoured if a marketing-intensive industry is entered, the investing firm is large, there are substantial intrasystem sales, and if the investing firm has much experience with operating in the host country. Further tests turned out that the variables included influence the firm's preferences more than its relative bargaining power. Several variables which had no significant impact on the firm's relative bargaining power were significant in previous studies (Fagre and Wells, 1982; Lecraw, 1984). In these studies, however, the two stages (firm preferences and bargaining power) were not distinguished and separated.

In a study on the foreign market entry modes of service firms, Erramilli (1991) expected to find a U-shaped relationship between the firms' desire for full control over foreign affiliates and their experience (both the length and the scope). In order to verify this U-shaped relationship, Erramilli mailed a survey to 463 US service firms involved in international operations, with a response rate of 44 per cent. Using logit analysis, the hypothesized U-shaped correlation between the level of control and the service firms' experience was confirmed. The length of experience turned out to be a more significant indicator of the entry mode selection than the scope of experience.

Based on transaction cost economics, Hennart (1991) examined whether Japanese manufacturing MNEs choose a WOS or a JV when entering the United States. He concentrated on costs and benefits of shared equity and added two other variables, viz. the concentration ratio of the industry entered, and the age of the subsidiary.[19] Hennart took a sample from a survey of Japanese affiliates in the US (Toyo Keizai Shinposha, 1987), which resulted in 158 observations. The empirical results of the logit models indicate that JVs are the preferred entry mode if the subsidiary is in a different industry than the Japanese MNE, the subsidiary is in a resource-based industry, or the Japanese MNE is entering a high-growth industry. Whenever the Japanese MNE's foreign experience increases or the subsidiary is older, WOSs are more likely.

Kim and Hwang (1992) tested their eclectic theory of the choice of international entry mode (Hill, Hwang, and Kim, 1990). They sent questionnaires to senior-level management of US-based MNEs, of which 137 were returned (a response rate of 22 per cent). The questions were used to calculate nine constructs, which were included in various statistical analyses (MANOVA, MDA, and multinominal logit analysis). In addition to JVs and WOSs, license arrangements were included in the testing as the base of reference. As a consequence, no direct comparisons were made between JVs and WOSs. The results of their logit analyses show that there is a significant positive relationship between the propensity to establish a WOS and all three strategic variables (global concentration, global synergies, and global strategic motivations), and the tacit nature of know-how. There is a significant negative relationship with country risk and location unfamiliarity. Moreover, their study revealed that there is a significant positive relationship between the preference for a JV and global synergies, global strategic motivations, and the tacit nature of know-how. However, a significant negative relationship was found with country risk and location unfamiliarity. This study largely supports their eclectic theory of the choice of international entry mode (Hill, Hwang, and Kim, 1990), and shows convincingly that besides variables from transaction cost economics and internalization theory, strategic variables should be included in the analysis of entry mode choices.

Agarwal and Ramaswami (1992a) investigated the impact of the OLI-advantages (Dunning, 1981, 1988) on the choice of the foreign-market servicing mode. Rather than including the extensive list of possible OLI advantages (see Dunning, 1981, 1988, 1993), Agarwal and Ramaswami used a manageable number of variables. As ownership advantages were taken: firm size, multinational experience, and the ability to develop differentiated products. Market potential and investment risk were the location advantages, while contractual risk was used as an internalization advantage. Besides testing the separate effects of the individual variables, they also formulated hypotheses on interactions between variables. In order to test the hypothesized effects, Agarwal and Ramaswami distributed a pre-tested questionnaire to the president or chief executive officer (CEO) of 536 American leasing firms, which led to a response rate of 23 per cent. Only 97 questionnaires were usable, each of which contained information on entries into three different countries: the UK, Japan, and Brazil. Four different options were considered: no involvement, exporting, JV, and WOS. After an exploratory factor analysis, a number of logit models were estimated. The results of the main effects indicated a preference for WOSs when firms are larger and more internationalized, and when investments are contemplated in markets with a high potential. The outcomes of the analyses of the interaction effects supported the joint hypotheses rather well. Larger and more internationalized firms prefer WOSs and JVs in low-potential countries, whereas smaller and less internationalized firms opt for JVs in high-potential markets. Furthermore, both JVs and WOSs are favoured over other modes of entry by firms with a higher ability to develop differentiated products when they deliberate investments in markets with higher contractual risks.

In a distinct study, Agarwal and Ramaswami (1992b) explored the choice between WOSs and JVs from a transaction cost perspective. Again, they tested separate and interaction effects. The main effects were the external and internal uncertainty firms encounter. In this study, external uncertainty concerned the host country's political and economic risk, while internal uncertainty involved the cultural distance between the home country and the host country. These main effects were also examined in interaction with firm size, multinational experience, and technological intensity. To test their hypotheses, Agarwal and Ramaswami collected data from publicly available sources on 148 foreign entries initiated by US manufacturing firms in the period 1985-1989. The logit analyses demonstrated an increased propensity towards WOSs in the case of higher external and lower internal uncertainty. Moreover, WOSs are favoured more by firms with little multinational experience than by firms with much multinational experience in a situation of external uncertainty. A similar conclusion is valid for the preference for JVs in the case of internal uncertainty (i.e., sociocultural distance).

In a study on the entry modes of Finnish firms, Larimo (1993) distinguished many possibly relevant variables. He conducted a survey of foreign entries made by Finnish manufacturing firms in OECD countries in the period 1977-1988. This approach resulted in 120 observations, which represents a response rate of 30 per cent. The logit analyses revealed that the probability of WOSs increases in proportion with the speed of internationalization, and the host country's economic size. JVs are more likely for larger firms, and for investments in resource-intensive industries.

Erramilli and Rao (1993) modified transaction cost economics to make it more suitable for explaining the entry mode choice of service firms. The authors claim that service firms always prefer maximum control when establishing a foreign entry mode. They added some strategic behaviour factors, such as global integration and market power, to transaction cost factors. Using data from the same survey as Erramilli (1991), which had a response rate of 44 per cent, the final sample consisted of 114 service firms with information on 381 foreign market entry choices. The logit analyses confirmed the expected pattern of influence only partially. JVs were found to be more likely in the case of high capital intensity, inseparable services, and a large cultural distance between the home country and the host country. In contrast, the propensity to establish WOSs increased with the level of asset specificity and the firm size.

Brouthers et al. (1993) placed a number of variables that were examined previously by various researchers into two categories: the desire for direct control and market complexity. They hypothesized that WOSs are more likely than JVs and contractual relationships (e.g., licensing and franchising) in the case of a higher desire for direct control. The opposite was expected for market complexity. To test these hypotheses, Brouthers and his colleagues collected data through a mail survey of 125 randomly selected American computer software firms. The response rate was 20 per cent. However, since the respondents were asked to fill in the questions for more entries, they received data on 72 observations. The ANOVA tests showed that both hypotheses were confirmed by the data.

Shane (1993) hypothesized that countries with a low power distance (see Hofstede, 1980) prefer JVs, while high power distant countries favour WOSs. To test this expectation, Shane used the Benchmark Surveys of 1977 and 1982, which together contain data on approximately 40,000 American foreign affiliates (see also Contractor, 1990b; Contractor and Lorange, 1988b). Contrary to the other empirical studies reviewed in this section, Shane used four different continuous dependent variables: the ratio of 50/50 and minority JVs to the total number of affiliates in 1977 and 1982, and the ratio of the sales of those JVs to the total sales of all affiliates in 1977 and 1982. Multiple regression analyses revealed that JVs are less likely than WOSs in countries which are characterized by a high power distance. Moreover, JVs appeared to have a positive relationship with restrictive policies of host governments, market size, and the level of uncertainty avoidance in the host country.

The next study was by Agarwal (1994), who investigated the relationship between cultural distance and the choice of JVs. He believed that a large cultural distance improves the chance that a JV is the selected entry mode. However, this effect is expected to be moderated by the multinational experience of firms, their technological intensity, their size, the riskiness of the host country, and the market potential. To test these hypotheses, Agarwal used the same sample as Agarwal and Ramaswami (1992b). The maximum likelihood estimations of the logit model confirmed the expected positive relationship between cultural distance and the incidence of JVs, and a negative relationship between the incidence of JVs and host-country risk and market potential. Furthermore, the level of multinational experience turned out to improve the likelihood that WOSs are initiated in countries with a large cultural distance.

Benito (1996) formulated some hypotheses based on both transaction cost economics and the behavioural approach (Cyert and March, 1963; Johanson and Vahlne, 1977; Johanson and Wiedersheim-Paul, 1975). He expected that WOSs are more likely if the firm's resource base is larger, specific assets are important, and if a firm has much international experience. High country risk and cultural distance increase the likelihood of JVs. The empirical data on foreign investments of Norwegian manufacturing firms were obtained from an existing survey conducted by the Norwegian Industrial Federation in 1984. The original sample of 254 foreign entries established by 104 firms was reduced to 174 observations, mainly because of missing data. The logit analyses corroborated the hypotheses that WOSs are preferred by larger firms, whereas JVs are favoured when host countries are judged as being risky, or diverge substantially from the home country's culture. Benito came to the conclusion that transaction cost economics appeared to be less relevant than behaviour-oriented variables in selecting foreign entry modes.

Madhok (1994) based his analyses on two important streams in the foreign entry literature: transaction cost economics and the organizational capability approach, which is comparable to resource-based perspectives. Madhok distributed a questionnaire to 750 senior executives of manufacturing MNEs based in North America and Europe. Exploratory factor analysis was used to create constructs for variables that were measured by multiple items. A response rate of 23 per cent was achieved. The number of observations was reduced to 130 observations because of missing data. Logit analyses showed that WOSs were favoured when firms are highly experienced in operating in international settings, and, in contrast with many other studies (e.g., Gatignon and Anderson, 1988; Kogut and Singh, 1988a), when the host and home countries have different cultures. Furthermore, the likelihood of JVs had a positive relationship with the experience with previous JVs, and the development of resources that may soon become obsolete in volatile environments. The main conclusion of this study was that transaction cost economics lost much of its relevance in the current dynamic environment which requires (global) strategic considerations and strategic behaviour (see Benito, 1996).

The last empirical study was by Padmanabhan and Cho (1994), who used data on 839 foreign subsidiaries of Japanese firms (Toyo Keizai Shinposha, 1992). The results of the logit analyses indicated that only four variables have a significant impact on Japanese foreign entry mode selection. Host-country experience, R&D intensity of the investing firms, and the cultural distance turned out to increase the odds that a WOS is set up. JVs were more likely when the host government follows a restrictive policy.

2.6 Conclusions

This chapter demonstrated that the selection of the appropriate mode of entry is a complex exercise, which is influenced by a great many factors. Nevertheless, firms should choose the right mode of entry, since they usually have only one real chance to become successful in the host country. Although there are many different possible modes of entry (see section 2.2), the focus of this study is on JVs and WOSs.

The comparison of relevant theoretical explanations of MNEs revealed that some theories, such as transaction cost economics, the strategic behaviour approach, resource-based theory, internalization theory, and the eclectic theory of Hill, Hwang, and Kim (1990) provide interesting viewpoints on the choice between JVs and WOSs. Elements of these theories are supported by empirical studies. The overview of relevant empirical studies on the choice between JVs and WOSs shows that the statistical tests in these studies (usually logit analysis) produced mixed results. Many variables turn out to have a significant impact on this choice. The overview clearly reveals that elements of the following theories are corroborated by empirical data:

1   transaction cost economics (see, e.g., Agarwal and Ramaswami, 1992b; Erramilli and Rao, 1993; Gatignon and Anderson, 1988; Hennart, 1991);
2   the strategic behaviour approach (see, e.g., Gomes-Casseres, 1989; Kim and Hwang, 1992, Madhok, 1994);
3   internalization theory (see, e.g., Agarwal and Ramaswami, 1992a; Gomes-Casseres, 1990; Shane, 1993);
4   the resource-based theory (see, e.g., Madhok, 1994);
5   Hill, Hwang, and Kim's eclectic theory (see Kim and Hwang, 1992).

The possible application of these theories in the conceptual framework of this study will be considered in the next chapter. That framework will serve as the basis for the formulation of hypotheses.

Notes

1   More recently, new terms have been introduced with more or less the same meaning, such as core competencies (Prahalad and Hamel, 1990) and core capabilities (Stalk, Evans, and Shulman, 1992).
2   In Porter's work, the choice of entry mode is hardly mentioned, although he is convinced that '... it is an important decision of the global competitor, ...' (Porter, 1986, p. 10).
3   Similar terms for this type of coordination are the 'buy' option (Richardson, 1972), 'spot market transactions' (Williamson, 1975, 1981), and 'open market transactions' (Root, 1987).
4   In many publications, barter and countertrade are entangled as it is believed that all forms of countertrade are directed at avoiding cash payments (Choudhry, McGeady, and Stiff, 1989; McVey, 1980; Mirus and Yeung, 1986, 1987). That is why countertrade is usually considered to be harmful for the present world trade (Halbach and Osterkamp, 1989; Lecraw, 1988, 1989).

5   This tendency is paradoxical because firms which have a leading position in the licensed technology sell their comparative advantage to their competitors. As a result, these firms risk losing their leading position.
6   There are, however, JVs in which one firm contributes part of its resources, while the partner firm brings in all of its resources. This particular type of JV can especially be found in relationships between large and small firms. Generally, smaller firms do not have enough managerial and financial resources to set up a JV in addition to their regular business.
7   See, for instance, Calvet (1981) and Dunning (1993) for a good overview of these macro- economic and financial theories.
8   Rugman (1979, 1981, 1985) goes one step further by claiming that internalization theory is a *general* theory of foreign direct investment.
9   Another name for this eclectic paradigm is OLI-paradigm, where OLI stands for ownership-specific advantages, location-specific advantages, and internalization incentive advantages, respectively (Dunning, 1988a, 1993).
10 See, for example, the classification proposed by Bain (1956): monopoly power, product differentiation, absolute cost barriers, and government interventions.
11 The fact that this article was written in French may be one of the reasons why it has been overlooked for more than two decades. Only recently, the concepts which were put forward by Hymer in this article are given the full credits they deserve (see, e.g., Dunning, 1993; Horaguchi and Toyne, 1990).
12 This 'automatic' way of generating revenues is in sharp contrast with the strategic behaviour approach which states that obtaining revenues depends on the strategic choices firms make.
13 Parry (1985) disputes the contention that internalization theory is a general theory of FDI, since it cannot provide explanations for the choice between exports, licensing and FDI, or for the existence of JVs.
14 These topics are treated extensively in the agency theory, which attempts to explain why organizations are structured as they are (see, e.g., Fama and Jensen, 1983). Central in this theory is the problem of aligning the firm's objectives with those of the agents (e.g., employees, managers, or foreign subsidiaries) such that self-interest-seeking behaviour is minimized.
15 Some of the studies presented investigated other modes of entry (e.g., licensing or acquisitions) in addition to JVs and WOSs.

16 The studies by Stopford and Wells (1972) and Kim and Hwang (1992) are not included in Table 2.1. The former study is excluded since no statistical tests were done, which makes it impossible to make statements on the level of significance. The latter study is left out because Kim and Hwang did not make a direct comparison between JVs and WOSs.
17 They, however, recognized that some of the variables included, such as cultural distance, are 'not central to transaction cost economics' (p. 311).
18 Stopford and Wells (1972) used a slightly different terminology. They referred to 'need for resources' rather than 'motivation for cooperation', and 'need for control' rather than 'organizational costs'.
19 This last variable was included since older JVs are more likely to be dissolved or acquired by one of the partners (compare Harrigan, 1985a; Killing, 1983).

3 Conceptual framework and hypotheses

This chapter contains the conceptual framework that will be used for analysing the choice between a JV and a WOS. Following previous eclectic studies (Agarwal and Ramaswami, 1992a; Hennart and Park, 1993; Hill, Hwang, and Kim, 1990; Kim and Hwang, 1992; Madhok, 1994), several theories will be combined to create a comprehensive framework. Based on this conceptual framework, a set of hypotheses will be formulated (section 3.2).

3.1 Conceptual framework

As stated in Chapter 1, the starting-point for building the conceptual framework of this study is the eclectic theory on the choice of foreign entry modes developed by Hill, Hwang, and Kim (1990). Using an eclectic framework is in line with real-world practice. The firm's business environment is affected by a great many different developments. The real world is so complex that it cannot be described adequately by one discipline alone. One-sided views are inappropriate for selecting the foreign entry mode, as this important strategic decision is influenced by many factors. Looking at this topic only with, for example, 'transaction cost eyes' may or will lead to neglecting other important (e.g., strategic) influences. Hence, a multidisciplinary or eclectic approach is required to obtain the most realistic descriptions.

Hill, Hwang, and Kim (1990) combined elements of the strategic behaviour approach, transaction cost economics, and internalization theory.[1] Each of these approaches is concerned with different issues which are only part of the story. The incorporation of these three theories is a good attribute of this eclectic model, for the following two reasons. First, as was demonstrated in section 2.4, the three approaches complement one another. The strategic behaviour approach concentrates on the competitive position of the firm as a whole, including both benefits and costs in the analysis. Transaction cost economics focuses on the transactional variables which determine the most efficient structure (in terms of costs) for governing individual transactions. Internalization theory uses the firm as the level of analysis, and adds the relevance of locational variables (compare Rugman and Verbeke, 1992, 1993b). These three complementary approaches together cover a broad range of topics which are important in foreign entry mode decisions. For instance, the peculiarities of the host country, the transaction, and the investing firm's strategy are explicitly taken into account. Firms which contemplate foreign expansion are definitely confronted with the constraints these topics pose on foreign investment. That is why they should be incorporated in a framework on foreign entry mode choices.

The second reason is that all three theories are empirically supported (see section 2.5). More specifically, the characteristics of individual transactions appear to affect the choice of foreign entry mode (see, e.g., Agarwal and Ramaswami, 1992b; Erramilli and Rao, 1993; Gatignon and Anderson, 1988; Hennart, 1991; Kim and Hwang, 1992). In a similar vein, the specific circumstances in the potential host country (see, e.g., Agarwal and Ramaswami, 1992a; Gomes-Casseres, 1990; Kim and Hwang, 1992) and the strategy of firms (Gomes-Casseres, 1989; Kim and Hwang, 1992; Madhok, 1994) turn out to have a decisive impact on the likelihood of a JV or a WOS.

An important shortcoming of Hill, Hwang, and Kim's eclectic theory is that it ignored the resource-based theory. This theory is focused on ownership-specific advantages like the utilization and enlargement of the firm's stock of resources and capabilities. Hence, it is oriented at internal organization. Given its focus and level of analysis (i.e., the organizational unit), this approach is complementary to the strategic behaviour approach, internalization theory, and transaction cost economics. For example, the complementarity of the resource-based theory and the strategic behaviour approach can be illustrated as follows: a firm's strategic flexibility is not only restricted by the firm's irreversible investments (i.e., strategic behaviour approach), but also by its stock of capabilities (Tallman, 1991; Teece, 1985). Another example is the development of a well-considered mixture of capabilities as a safeguard against contextual fluctuations, which enables the firm to improve its competitive position (Madhok, forthcoming). As a consequence, the resource-based theory provides valuable insights into foreign entry mode choices, and, therefore, deserves to be included in a framework on this topic. Moreover, empirical research corroborates the relevance of the resource-based theory for the choice between a JV and a WOS (see Madhok, 1994).

In the present study, the relevance of the resource-based theory is acknowledged. As a consequence, this theory will be incorporated in Hill, Hwang, and Kim's framework, which serves as the basis for the conceptual framework of this study. Before elaborating this framework, it will be explained why the other approaches that were distinguished in Chapter 2 (Hymer's theory and Dunning's eclectic paradigm) are not included in the framework.

Hymer's market imperfections theory uses monopolistic advantages in explaining the existence of MNEs. However, in the present turbulent business environment, monopolistic advantages are no longer realistic sources of profit. Furthermore, this theory merely accepts cooperative forms of organization (such as JVs), without attempting to give clear reasons for their existence. These two attributes make that Hymer's theory is not suitable for inclusion in a framework for the choice between a JV and a WOS.

Although Dunning (1981, 1988, 1993) postulated some very interesting ideas on internationalization (e.g., the distinction between three groups of advantages: ownership, location, and internalization), his approach is not applicable in this study either. The focus of his eclectic paradigm is on explaining why the whole population of MNEs has developed cross-border activities. This focus deviates substantially from the goal of the present study, which is to determine and, if possible, predict the factors that actually influence an individual firm's foreign entry mode choice. Moreover, Dunning's eclectic paradigm leans quite heavily on monopolistic advantages, which was the main reason to exclude Hymer's theory.

Thus, four complementary approaches remain regarding the choice between a JV and a WOS: the strategic behaviour approach, internalization theory, transaction cost economics, and the resource-based theory. These approaches are combined into a unifying framework. The relevant approaches differ from one another with regard to, for example, the underlying assumptions, the units of analysis, and the respective viewpoints. This makes a full integration of the four approaches unfeasible. Therefore, an *eclectic* framework will be created, which, by definition, links only those parts of theories that are consistent with one another (see Noorderhaven, 1995).

```
                    Strategic Behaviour Approach
                                |
                                |      HHK
                                ↓
    Resource-           foreign           Trans-
    Based      →        entry    ←        action
    Theory              mode              Cost
                        choice            Economics     OLI
                           ↑
                           |
                    Internalization Theory
                                              Hymer's
                                              Theory
```

HHK = Hill, Hwang and Kim's eclectic theory of foreign entry mode choices
OLI = Dunning's eclectic paradigm

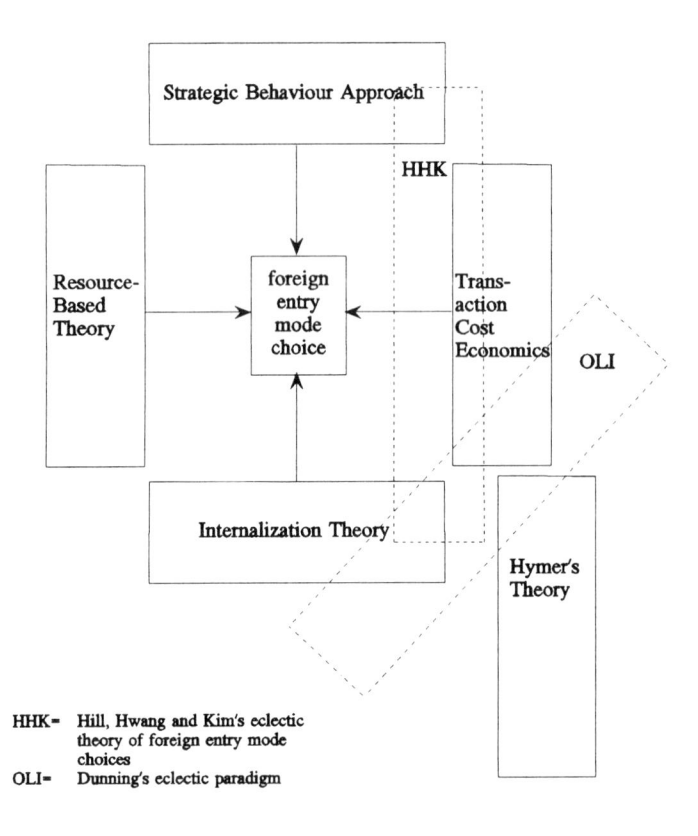

Figure 3.1 Schematic presentation of the ability of theoretical approaches to provide explanations for foreign entry mode choice (JVs versus WOSs)

The results of the discussion in this section and in section 2.4 are summarized in Figure 3.1. This figure shows that four theoretical approaches (the strategic behaviour approach, transaction cost economics, internalization theory, and the resource-based theory) can provide (partial) explanations for the foreign entry mode choice. In contrast, Hymer's market imperfections theory cannot explain which foreign entry mode will be chosen. Hill, Hwang, and Kim's eclectic theory combines elements of three of these relevant theories: the strategic behaviour approach, transaction cost economics, and internalization theory. As such, it is able to link three partial explanations. Dunning's OLI paradigm includes parts of Hymer's theory, transaction cost economics, and internalization theory. This paradigm cannot adequately predict the mode of foreign entry, as it is partially based on Hymer's theory, which is irrelevant for foreign entry mode choices. An additional reason is that it is focused on the level of all MNEs rather than on the level of the individual firm.

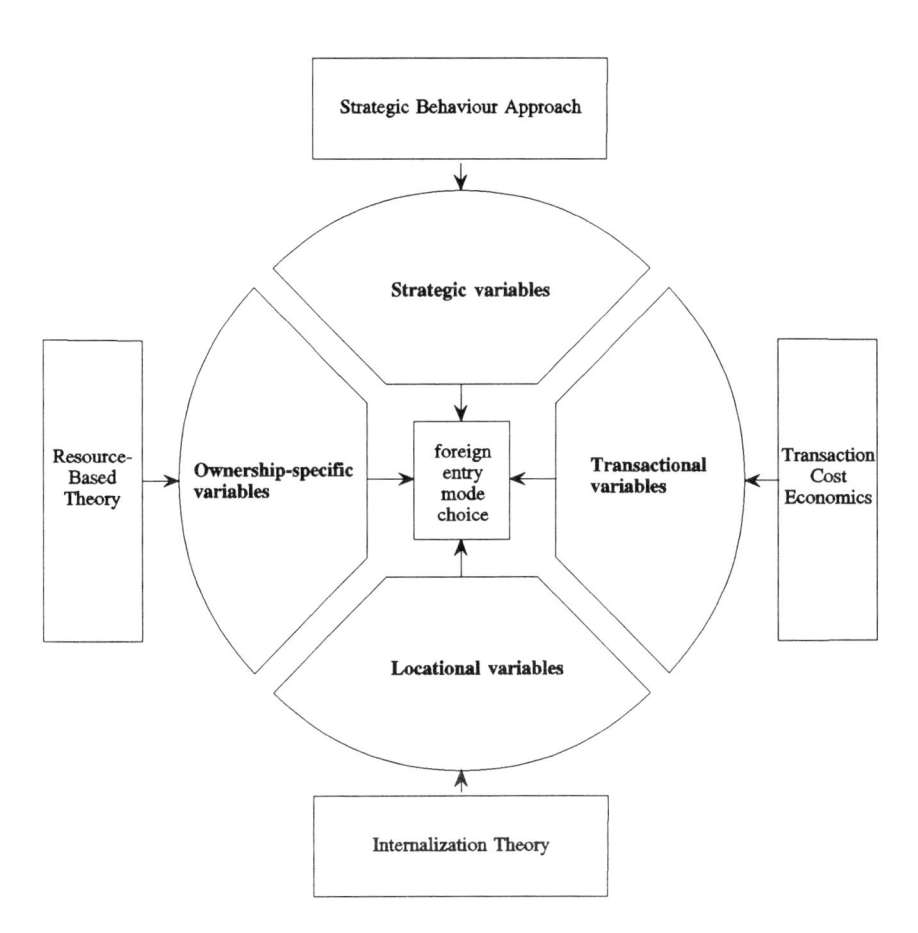

Figure 3.2 The conceptual framework of the comprehensive eclectic theory of the foreign entry mode choice

In the present study, a more comprehensive framework will be used: all four theories that produce partial explanations for the foreign entry mode choice are integrated. Thus, the strategic behaviour approach, transaction cost economics, internalization theory, and the resource-based theory are incorporated in the conceptual framework. Following Hill, Hwang, and

Kim (1990), three groups of variables are distinguished that influence the foreign entry mode choice: strategic variables, transactional variables, and locational variables. These groups of variables are closely related to the strategic behaviour approach, to transaction cost economics, and to internalization theory, respectively. However, the present study added the resource-based theory to Hill, Hwang, and Kim's eclectic theory, which implies that a fourth group of variables (ownership-specific variables) needs to be distinguished. This group of variables, which contains the firm-specific capabilities and resources, has a direct link with the resource-based theory. Figure 3.2 presents the conceptual framework. This framework is the basis for the formulation of the hypotheses in the next section.

3.2 Hypotheses

Below, hypotheses will be formulated for each group of variables.

Strategic variables

MNEs may pursue a *multi-domestic strategy* or a *global strategy* (Hout, Porter, and Rudden, 1982). A multi-domestic strategy is based on the notion that national markets differ with regard to, for instance, local habits, preferences of customers, and political and social structures. In order to increase the probability of success, firms have to adjust, among other things, their products, their marketing policy, their management style, and their way of influencing the relevant stakeholders to the local circumstances. To establish a perfect fit between the local conditions and the firms' strategy and behaviour, local subsidiaries should receive as much control as required to operate autonomously. Attempts by MNE's headquarters to determine the particular decisions local subsidiaries should make, will inevitably lead to an insufficient or even an incorrect level of local responsiveness (Bartlett and Ghoshal, 1989). Generally, headquarters are not informed well enough to fully understand the peculiarities of local regions where the MNE is actively involved. That is why a decentralized approach is preferred. Decentralization and delegation of authority and responsibilities imply that the MNE has only limited control over the local affiliates. It should be stressed that becoming acquainted with the specific local culture and environment is a time-consuming process. The knowledge needed is of a tacit nature, which necessitates the relationship with a local firm (e.g., a JV).

A global strategy is more or less the opposite of a multi-domestic strategy, in the sense that equality of preferences and markets is expected to exist. A global strategy implies that an MNE attempts to gain economies of scale by concentrating production in one country (or a limited number of countries) and by exporting its products worldwide (Bartlett and Ghoshal, 1989; Ghoshal, 1987). These global economies of scale form the firm's non-location-bound firm-specific advantages (Rugman and Verbeke, 1993b). A certain degree of centralized coordination is required to take maximum advantage of the economies of scale (Bartlett and Ghoshal, 1989; Hout, Porter, and Rudden, 1982). Only then, MNEs are able to avoid that subsidiaries maximize their own performance at the expense of the performance of other subsidiaries. Suboptimization may harm the MNE's competitive position and overall performance. Hence, full control is required in the case of a global strategy to minimize the risk of cannibalism and suboptimization (Hill, Hwang, and Kim, 1990).

So far, only one study (Kim and Hwang, 1992) investigated the effect of strategy on the foreign entry mode choice. Kim and Hwang found that, in the case of a global strategy, firms prefer setting up either WOSs or JVs to licensing. Unfortunately, they did not differentiate between WOSs and JVs.

The above discussion leads to the first hypothesis of this study:

H1 A global strategy decreases the likelihood of JVs

A second strategic variable that is believed to influence the foreign entry mode selection process is the *level of competition* in the industry entered. When competition is intensive, a WOS is not a suitable mode of entry as it creates additional capacity. The incumbent firms will not accept an intruder in their industry without any resistance. Strategic reactions, such as price reduction, the creation of idle capacity, and collusion can be expected as expressions of retaliation (Hennart and Park, 1994). In this regard, it is important that the entering firm's strategic flexibility is guaranteed (Harrigan, 1985b, 1985c). Only then, a quick and immediate response to the counteractions of the incumbent firms is possible (e.g., a fast exit). Therefore, firms should not commit many resources as this restricts their flexibility.

In contrast, a JV with an incumbent firm usually creates hardly any additional capacity if the existing capacity of that firm is to be utilized. This relative advantage of JVs increases the propensity to establish JVs in highly competitive industries (see Hill, Hwang, and Kim, 1990). Several studies tested this hypothesis, but failed to find a significant effect (Hennart, 1991; Kim and Hwang, 1992; Kogut and Singh, 1988b). Only Gomes-Casseres (1990) was able to confirm that the level of competition has a positive influence on the probability of JVs being set up.

H2 Strong competition in the industry entered increases the likelihood of JVs

The last strategic variable investigated in this study is the *growth of the industry*. If a subsidiary's industry is growing rapidly, MNEs may use an incumbent partner to gain a better competitive position faster (Kogut and Singh, 1988b). The creation of a WOS may be too time consuming to benefit from the increased market opportunities. Alternatively, JVs with incumbent firms can be set up much more rapidly, because, at least, part of the production capacity is already available. Therefore, JVs offer better prospects than WOSs in fast-growing industries. However, this statement is only valid if the disadvantage of sharing profits with the JV partner is smaller than the time disadvantage of setting up a WOS. Hennart (1991) investigated the effect of industry growth on the choice of entry mode. He found that JVs are more likely to be set up than WOSs in case a subsidiary's industry is growing rapidly.

H3 High growth in the industry entered increases the likelihood of JVs

Ownership-specific variables

Below, four different types of experience (i.e., firm-specific capabilities) and one resource (i.e., the relative size) will be considered.

When firms cross their national borders for the first time, they do not know how to deal with all kinds of uncertainties and foreign peculiarities. They are, for instance, not familiar with foreign norms and values, foreign legislation, other foreign requirements, the preferences of foreign customers, and the best way to bargain with foreign governments. This lack of knowledge may be neutralized by forming a JV with a firm that possesses the knowledge required.

Over time, firms learn how to deal with unknown situations. They gain experience in managing external and internal uncertainty, and learn how to reduce risks to proper proportions (compare, Barkema, Bell, and Pennings, 1996; Cyert and March, 1963; Johanson and Vahlne, 1977; Johanson and Wiedersheim-Paul, 1975). Empirical research revealed that international experience has a positive effect on the likelihood of FDI (see, e.g., Terpstra and Yu, 1988; Yu, 1990). Firms with much international experience know how to operate in various contexts and, thus, do not need a partner firm. This finding is confirmed in several empirical studies (Agarwal and Ramaswami, 1992a, 1992b; Benito, 1996; Gatignon and Anderson, 1988; Madhok, 1994). The results of some other studies, however, turned out to be insignificant (Larimo, 1993; Padmanabhan and Cho, 1994).

Erramilli (1991) investigated the foreign entry mode choices of service firms, and discovered a curve-linear (U-shaped) relationship between the firm's multinational experience and its preference for WOSs. This outcome indicates that both unexperienced and highly experienced firms favour WOSs to JVs. Erramilli supposed that less experienced firms are eager to fully control their activities because of an ethnocentric orientation,[2] or to prevent problems with transaction partners. There is some additional evidence that firms with little international experience prefer to have a high level of control over their foreign ventures (Davidson and McFetridge, 1985; Shetty, 1979; Stopford and Wells, 1972). Notwithstanding these findings, most evidence points to a generally positive relationship between the foreign experience of firms and their tendency to opt for WOSs. Hence, the following hypothesis is formulated:

H4   Much international experience decreases the likelihood of JVs

A similar argument applies to the *host country experience* of firms (Gomes-Casseres, 1989, 1990; Hennart, 1991; Kim and Hwang, 1992). Firms that are very experienced in operating in a particular country are familiar with the local peculiarities, which increases the chance of new FDIs (Davidson, 1980; Yu, 1990). They know, for instance, how to deal with the indigenous population, the local authorities, the cultural differences, the employees, the clients, and so on. As a result, such firms do not need the specific knowledge about local conditions that local firms usually possess. Less experienced firms lack country-specific information which cannot be obtained easily in a limited period of time, unless a partnership with a local firm is established.

Various studies confirm that firms which are experienced in operating in the host country will expand more likely by means of a WOS than via a JV (Gomes-Casseres, 1989, 1990; Hennart, 1991; Padmanabhan and Cho, 1994). In Larimo's study (1993), the outcome of this proposed effect did not satisfy the requirements of statistical significance.

H5   Much host country experience decreases the likelihood of JVs

A third firm-specific capability which may have a bearing on the foreign entry mode choice, is the firm's *mode experience*, or, more precisely, the experience a firm has with previous JVs or WOSs. The idea behind incorporating this variable is that learning from earlier mode experiences may affect a next entry mode decision. Negative experiences with a specific mode of entry reduce the probability that the same mode will be selected again in the future, whereas in the case of positive experiences the opposite may apply.

JVs are more complex to manage than WOSs because the interests of at least two firms are involved (Bell, 1993b; Harrigan, 1985a; Killing, 1983; Lorange and Roos, 1991). At the same time, different corporate cultures, which have to be matched to prevent misunderstandings and unnecessary problems, come together in one new entity. The international context may aggravate the effects of intercultural differences (Buckley and Casson, 1988). Frequently, the partners' interests conflict with each other, which may cause frictions. Especially 50/50 JVs are susceptible to all kinds of problems, since the partners are involved in the decision-making process on an equal basis. Such problems range from a delay to a block in decision making, and may even lead to a termination of the venture (Killing, 1983). However, firms which previously established JVs will have learnt how to deal with alien corporate cultures, negotiations with potential partners, the transfer of knowledge, and the complexities of managing JVs (Lyles, 1988; Mody, 1993; Shetty, 1979; Tallman and Shenkar, 1994; Westney, 1988). Such firms are expected to have a preference for JVs when a new entry decision is made.

A similar argument can be presented for previous experiences in managing WOSs. Madhok (1994) investigated the effects of mode experience on the entry mode choice. His study confirmed that the propensity to set up JVs increases with the firms' experience with JVs. Experience with WOSs turned out to have no significant impact on the incidence of WOSs. Although only the first relationship is supported by previous empirical research, a hypothesis will be formulated for both effects.

H6a Much JV experience increases the likelihood of JVs

H6b Much WOS experience increases the likelihood of WOSs

The last capability considered in this study is *product experience*. This variable concerns the experience a firm has with the foreign subsidiary's core products. When firms engage in product markets outside their core business, they often lack the specific knowledge of the activities to become successful. Frequently, firms have no access to distribution channels for products outside their core business. The impact of these deficiencies is stronger when diversification takes place outside the home country. Then, firms will have to make use of the skills and knowledge of one or more other firms, since the skills, knowledge, and access required cannot be learnt or acquired easily. In this case, a JV will be the most efficient mode to obtain these assets (e.g., through learning by doing) (Hennart, 1991).[3] In contrast, when new activities are more comparable with or even similar to the current core activities, firms do not need the inputs from other firms. Then, firms will prefer full control to shared control (Gomes-Casseres, 1985; Hennart, 1991).

The relationship between product or activity inexperience and the propensity to set up JVs is confirmed by several empirical studies (e.g., Gomes-Casseres, 1985; Hennart, 1991; Hennart and Reddy, 1992; Stopford and Wells, 1972; Zejan, 1988). Other studies, however, found an insignificant effect (Gomes-Casseres, 1989; Larimo, 1993; Padmanabhan and Cho, 1994). A somewhat different analysis was made by Madhok (1994). He did not investigate the separate impact of the activity experience, but only the interaction of that variable with the volatility of the environment. The underlying reason for this interaction is that Madhok, following March (1991), believes that learning effects become less useful in turbulent contexts. Thus, over time the relevance of experience with products will become less in volatile environments. Although his argument seems valid, his approach will not be incorporated in this study, since this would imply that all hypotheses regarding some kind of experience should include the volatility of the environment. Given the substantial amount of confirmation, the following hypothesis will be formulated:

H7 Much product experience decreases the likelihood of JVs

In addition to these capabilities, one ownership-specific resource will be examined: the relative size of the foreign affiliate.

If the subsidiary is large compared to the MNE, the MNE presumably lacks financial and managerial resources to run the subsidiary on its own (Contractor and Lorange, 1988b; Harrigan, 1985a). In that case, a partner firm is needed to achieve the goals intended. The partner may provide the money, time, and personnel to ensure the necessary fit between needs and resources. Without that correspondence, the goals of the foreign affiliate and the intentions of the investing firm will not be realized. If no suitable partner firm can be found, the investing firm will have to refrain from its plans to invest abroad. Alternatively, the subsidiary will not receive the attention and the funding it needs to become successful.

Some empirical studies examined the impact of the relative size of the foreign subsidiary on the foreign entry mode choice. Only one study (Kogut and Singh, 1988b) corroborates the relationship between the relative size and the propensity to establish a JV. Two other studies failed to find significant effects (Hennart, 1991; Larimo, 1993).

H8   Relatively large investments increase the likelihood of JVs

Transactional variables

When a firm transfers *specific assets* to its subsidiaries (e.g., proprietary technological or marketing know-how, or specific skills regarding quality control), that firm will be inclined to prevent a decrease in the value of those specific assets. An essential feature of these transaction-specific assets is that they cannot be utilized, or only at very high costs, in different transactions. Consequently, there is a real danger of becoming locked in in the transactional relationship (Williamson, 1975, 1985). Therefore, firms will be anxious to internalize transactions which are characterized by specific investments. This preference will be stronger if the risk of opportunistic behaviour of other firms is high. WOSs provide better safeguards against the risk of the dissemination of know-how than JVs, as in the latter case there are always at least two parties involved, with possibly deviating interests (Buckley and Casson, 1976; Gatignon and Anderson, 1988; Hennart, 1988). In WOSs, top management can use authority and rules to prevent or minimize opportunistic behaviour (Williamson, 1975, 1985). However, these mechanisms do not work perfectly. Even within the hierarchical governance structure, transaction costs exist because of potential opportunistic behaviour (Hennart, 1982). Thus, firms will prefer full control over their affiliates if the risk of opportunistic behaviour regarding the transferred assets is high.

In contrast, if the risk of opportunistic behaviour is low or even negligible (e.g., in situations characterized by mutual trust, mutual forbearance, and mutual commitment) highly specific assets could also be transferred by means of a JV (Beamish and Banks, 1987; Buckley and Casson, 1988).

Many empirical studies examined the specificity of the transferred assets, although the measurement of this variable varies. Frequently, the research and development (R&D) intensity of the investing firm was used as a proxy. Gatignon and Anderson (1988) and Padmanabhan and Cho (1994) found a significant positive effect of the R&D intensity on the preference for a WOS. In some other studies insignificant results were obtained (Agarwal, 1994; Agarwal and Ramaswami, 1992b;

Benito, 1996; Davidson and McFetridge, 1985; Fagre and Wells, 1982; Hennart, 1991; Larimo, 1993; Stopford and Wells, 1972). Whenever the R&D intensity of the subsidiary was used as measure for asset specificity, it appeared that the incidence of JVs increased as opposed to WOSs (Gomes-Casseres, 1989; Kogut and Singh, 1988a, 1988b). Two studies attempted to measure the asset specificity with a survey (Erramilli and Rao, 1993; Madhok, 1994). Only the former found a positive and significant impact of asset specificity on the propensity to set up WOSs. In sum, most of the evidence points to the relationship hypothesized by H9:

H9 The transfer of highly specific assets decreases the likelihood of JVs

The *reputation* of the expanding firm may also affect the choice of the foreign mode of entry. Firms must invest heavily in advertising and their brand name to obtain a good reputation. This process of reputation building is time consuming and uncertain. High investments in reputation do not automatically lead to a good reputation. Each minor deviation from the behaviour that the firm prescribes may have a disastrous impact on the firm's reputation. Therefore, firms that invest heavily in brand-name capital will try to avoid free riding by other firms (Brickley and Dark, 1987; Caves, 1982). Free riding means that a firm takes advantage of the reputation of another firm without bearing any costs (Anderson and Gatignon, 1986). The former firm may earn high short-term profits by making low-quality products, and sell them under the brand name of the latter firm. As a result, the firm's reputation will deteriorate. High-control entry modes are considered to be the most efficient governance structures in situations where the risk of free riding is high (Brickley and Dark, 1987; Caves, 1982; Williamson, 1985).

This expected relation was explored in several empirical studies. Gatignon and Anderson (1988) and Stopford and Wells (1972) found a positive, significant impact of the investing firm's advertising intensity on the propensity to establish WOSs. The results of Hennart's study (1991) revealed an insignificant relationship. In some other studies, the marketing intensity of the subsidiary was taken as a measure for the firm's reputation. Gomes-Casseres (1989, 1990) found evidence for the proposed effect, whereas Kogut and Singh (1988a, 1988b) only obtained insignificant results.

H10 A good reputation decreases the likelihood of JVs

Locational variables

Four locational variables are distinguished: the difference between the home country's culture and the host country's culture, the riskiness of the host country, the host government's policy towards FDI, and the level of welfare in the host country. For all variables a hypothesis will be formulated.

The *cultural difference* between the home country and the host country may entail many difficulties for firms that contemplate foreign entry. The larger the cultural difference is, the larger the problems are. MNEs are unfamiliar with local norms, values, and traditions, when an investment is made in culturally dissimilar countries. In such cases, MNEs will probably encounter many situations of miscomprehension, because of their lack of knowledge about the precise cultural backgrounds. For example, an MNE may unintendedly offend local authorities or clients by acting and behaving in a way different from what is expected. This may cause frustration and irritation on the side of the local parties, which may eventually lead to an overt opposition to entry and the MNE's presence in the local market. As a consequence, the MNE may fail to achieve its goals, and may have to consider premature withdrawal from the market.

In order to prevent or, at least, minimize the repercussions of cultural divergence, firms will have to become acquainted with the relevant aspects of the host country's culture. Since the knowledge required is tacit, it cannot be acquired easily. Setting up a WOS from scratch to become acquainted with local culture is a time-consuming path paved with many obstacles. A much faster way of getting acquainted with the norms, values, expected behaviour, and habits of the host country is to establish a JV with a local firm (Gatignon and Anderson, 1988; Kogut and Singh, 1988a). Then, the local partner can explain the underlying concepts, and train the foreign MNE in this area. Hence, a positive relationship between national cultural dissimilarity and the propensity to form JVs is expected.

Similarly, a hypothesis can be introduced with regard to cultural similarity. In many publications on JVs, it is stressed that JV partners should have a comparable cultural background to make the relationship successful (see, e.g., Bell, 1993b; Brown, Rugman, and Verbeke, 1989; Buckley and Casson, 1988; Harrigan, 1985, 1986; Hennart, 1988; Kogut, 1988; Lorange and Roos, 1991, 1992). This suggests that JVs are the appropriate mode of entry in countries with a national culture that is comparable to the home country's culture.

The two theoretical perspectives do not exclude each other. Empirical research supports the use of JVs in culturally distant countries (e.g., Agarwal, 1994; Agarwal and Ramaswami, 1992b; Benito, 1996; Davidson, 1982; Erramilli, 1991; Erramilli and Rao, 1993; Gatignon and Anderson, 1988; Gomes-Casseres, 1985; Kogut and Singh, 1988a)[4], but also the opposite (Madhok, 1994; Padmanabhan and Cho, 1994). Given the mixed support, no specific effect was hypothesized for the relationship between the entry mode choice and the cultural distance:

H11 The cultural distance between the home country and the host country influences the likelihood of JVs

The *riskiness of the host country* is believed to be a significant determinant of the foreign entry mode choice. When a country's political, legal, cultural, and economic environment is uncertain and unpredictable, MNEs should not commit themselves too much as they may loose their strategic flexibility (Gatignon and Anderson, 1988; Harrigan, 1985a, 1985c; Kim and Hwang, 1992). This contextual risk (Root, 1988) is usually beyond the control of firms. Even if a WOS is established, firms will not be able to really control the uncertainties and to minimize the inherent negative consequences, such as opportunistic behaviour. Moreover, in risky countries the host government may nationalize the properties owned by foreign firms. Hence, the amount of loss possible should be kept as low as possible. A proper means for this is to form a JV with a local firm, since the risk of nationalization and possible xenophobic reactions will be lower when a local firm is involved in the business operation.

Mixed results were obtained in empirical studies. A number of studies confirmed that high-control entry modes are not very likely in the case of risky host countries (see, e.g., Benito, 1996; Gatignon and Anderson, 1988; Kim and Hwang, 1992), whereas in other studies the opposite was found (Agarwal, 1994; Agarwal and Ramaswami, 1992b). Research by Erramilli and Rao (1993) revealed that WOSs are preferred over JVs as modes of entry in risky host countries, if the assets to be transferred to the foreign subsidiary are characterized by a high level of specificity. This study expects that country risk has a positive effect on the incidence of JVs.

H12 Host country risk increases the likelihood of JVs

Another factor that may have a substantial impact on the foreign entry mode choice is the *host government policy* on FDI. Certain governments put restrictions on the ownership of local activities by foreign MNEs; for instance, 100 per cent foreign ownership of local subsidiaries is not allowed. In that case, foreign ownership is only possible if a local firm owns part of the shared equity. WOSs are, thus, no longer a viable mode of entry, which obviously increases the propensity to form (minority) JVs with local firms (compare Franko, 1989).

However, in spite of the restricting rules, some MNEs are able to establish WOSs because they have a good bargaining position as compared to the foreign government. A firm's bargaining position depends, among other things, on the type of technology that will be transferred to the host country and the number of potential rival firms that can provide the same assets (Fagre and Wells, 1982; Gomes-Casseres, 1990; Lecraw, 1984). When a firm's products are new and innovative, the firm's bargaining position is better than when products become more mature (Bivens and Lovell, 1966; Davidson, 1982). This effect is called the 'obsolescing bargain' (Vernon, 1977). Since only a few MNEs may be able to build up enough bargaining power to circumvent the requirements of the host government, most firms have to adjust to the rules imposed. Therefore, it is postulated that JVs are the preferred entry mode when host governments restrict foreign ownership. Previous research strongly corroborated this relationship (Gatignon and Anderson, 1988; Gomes-Casseres, 1989, 1990; Padmanabhan and Cho, 1994; Shane, 1993).

Here, it should be stressed that governments are recognizing more and more that restricting foreign ownership is not always the best solution for their countries. Therefore, nearly all restrictive governments (such as India, Indonesia, Mexico, China, Japan, France) relinquished their restrictive policies towards foreign investments in the last decade (Contractor, 1990b).

H13 A restrictive host government policy increases the likelihood of JVs

The last hypothesis of this study concerns the *level of welfare* in the host country. This variable is meant to indicate the attractiveness of a country to serve as a potential market for selling products. A high level of welfare suggests that the country is well developed. Obviously, this has a substantial impact on, for instance, the level of education of the indigenous population, the buying power of people, and the capabilities of local firms. Therefore, it can be expected that setting up a JV with a local firm would be beneficial for MNEs, since these firms have something to offer, such as good craftsmanship, technological know-how, marketing know-how, and so on. An additional advantage is that, because of the high level of education, enough qualified employees can be hired.

A number of studies confirmed the greater likelihood of JVs in the case of a high level of welfare (Gomes-Casseres, 1989, 1990; Kobrin, 1987; Larimo, 1993; Shane, 1993), although others found the opposite relationship (Agarwal, 1994; Agarwal and Ramaswami, 1992a, 1992b). Nevertheless, it is hypothesized that:

H14   The level of welfare in the host country increases the likelihood of JVs

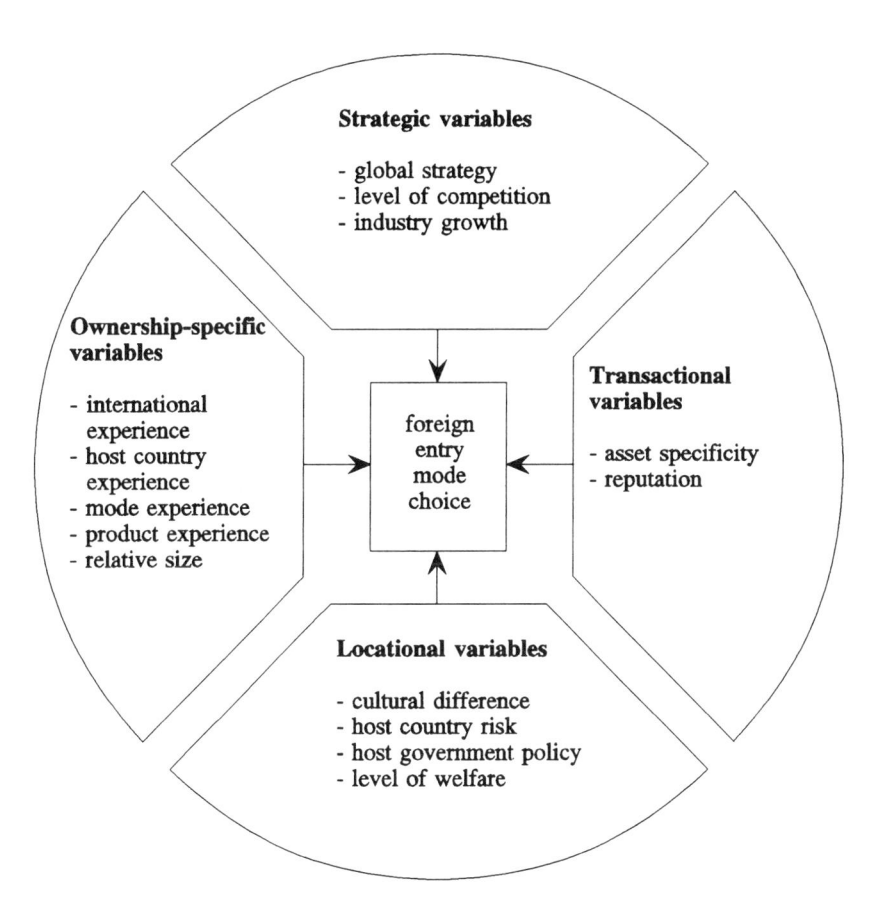

Figure 3.3 The four groups of variables that influence the foreign entry mode choice

3.3 Conclusions

In this chapter, a comprehensive, eclectic conceptual framework was built that will be used in the present study. The framework is mainly based on four theoretical approaches: the strategic behaviour approach, the resource-based theory, transaction cost economics, and internalization theory. Four relevant groups of variables were distinguished: strategic variables, ownership-specific variables, transactional variables, and locational variables (see Figure 3.3). For each variable a hypothesis was formulated (see Table 3.1). In the next chapter, the methodology of the empirical part of this study will be presented.

Table 3.1
Overview of the hypothesized effects of the variables on the choice between a JV and a WOS

VARIABLES	EXPECTED INFLUENCE (+ = JV)
investing firm's strategy	−
level of competition	+
industry growth	+
international experience	−
host country experience	−
JV experience	+
WOS experience	−
product experience	−
relative size of foreign affiliate	+
level of asset specificity	−
investing firm's reputation	−
cultural difference	?
host country risk	+
restrictive host government policy	+
level of welfare in host country	+

Notes

1 They, however, did not explicitly report that they wanted to combine the insights of these three approaches.

2   An ethnocentric orientation means that a firm prefers to have its own people or people from its home country in the most important positions with a foreign venture. Japanese firms generally have such an ethnocentric orientation.
3   Another argument which fits more within the strategic behaviour approach is that firms are often not willing to invest large sums of money in activities that lie outside their core business. Possible reasons are the lack of in-depth knowledge of the peculiarities of the products involved, the inability to assess the risk in different contexts, and the observation that non-core activities usually receive less attention than core activities.
4   Firms with much international experience, however, prefer WOSs over JVs in the case of more cultural distance (Agarwal, 1994; Agarwal and Ramaswami, 1992b).

4 Methodology

The conceptual framework that was built in the previous chapter led to a number of hypotheses that will be tested empirically. This chapter describes the methodology that is used to test these hypotheses. The process of data collection is explained in section 4.1, and the operationalization of the variables in section 4.2. A description of the sample is given in section 4.3, and the statistical techniques used in section 4.4. The last section contains some concluding remarks.

4.1 Data collection

Most previous empirical studies on foreign entry mode choices used existing (i.e., secondary) data for testing hypotheses. A prominent source is the Harvard Multinational Enterprise database, which contains data on more than 19,000 foreign subsidiaries of 180 large US MNEs from 1900 to 1975 (see Curhan, Davidson, and Suri, 1977). Several researchers were allowed to use this enormous database for statistical analyses (e.g., Chowdhury, 1992; Davidson, 1980; Davidson and McFetridge, 1985; Gatignon and Anderson, 1988; Gomes-Casseres, 1987, 1989, 1990). Other researchers built their own databases using data from governmental and/or commercial institutions (e.g., Agarwal, 1994; Cho and Padmanabhan, 1995; Hennart, 1991; Hennart and Park, 1993, 1994; Kogut and Singh, 1988a, 1988b; Padmanabhan and Cho, 1994; Shane, 1994). Although using existing data is fairly popular, it has recently been acknowledged that survey data are a promising alternative (see Agarwal and Ramaswami, 1992a; Benito, 1996; Erramilli, 1991; Kim and Hwang, 1992; Larimo, 1993). The reason is that archival data do not contain direct information on underlying motives. Surveys offer the opportunity to gain insight into the perceptions of decision makers and the factors that influence the mode selection.

The present study recognizes the importance of measuring perceptions in (strategic) decision making (compare Noorderhaven, 1995). Decision makers base their decisions not only on objective data, but also on their subjective judgments. Suppose, for example, that a country is considered to be a risky country according to objective criteria. Then, a JV is the more likely mode of entry than a WOS. However, when the decision maker perceives a country as not risky at all, he or she will probably select a WOS to be the entry mode. Hence, it is crucial to know how decision makers perceive their internal and external environments.

Several techniques can be used for collecting subjective or perceptual data, e.g., surveys, interviews, and observations (see Mintzberg, 1973; Yin, 1989). Surveys are especially appropriate for large-scale studies, interviewing and observing being too time consuming and, consequently, too expensive to be employed in such studies. As indicated in Chapter 1, this study is directed at gaining insight into the factors that influence the choice between a JV and a WOS. A cross-sectional approach was followed to obtain data on potentially influencing factors. To increase the external validity of the results, it was attempted to obtain many observations. Since surveys are appropriate methods of collecting perceptual data on a large scale, a survey was conducted in the present study.

Although surveys appear to be easy to use, there are many caveats. Some of the potential problems are: questions can be interpreted in multiple ways, terms used may be misunderstood by respondents, the response rate may be (too) low, and respondents may be guided towards outcomes ex-ante preferred by the researcher (see, e.g., Babbie, 1990; Churchill, 1991).

In contrast with most previous studies, data were collected both at the level of the firm and at the level of the individual entry. Such data are more informative about the exact internal and external situations at the time of entry than data at the level of the industry only, which were used by previous researchers (e.g., Caves and Mehra, 1986; Davidson and McFetridge, 1985; Gatignon and Anderson, 1988; Gomes-Casseres, 1989; Kogut and Singh, 1988a).

The questionnaire contained questions about the firm and questions about foreign JVs and WOSs. The only difference between the questions concerning JVs and the questions about WOSs was that, in the former case, some questions about the division of equity and control were included. Many questions required the respondent to score on a 7-point Likert-type scale. In some cases, the extremes ranged from 'very good' to 'very bad', and in other cases from 'very large' to 'very small', depending on the questions. In addition, a number of questions with two categories (e.g., yes/no) and some open-ended questions were included. The main reasons for the focus on questions with limited response categories rather than on open-ended questions were the greater uniformity of responses and, thus, the relative ease of data processing (Babbie, 1990). The questionnaire is given in Appendix A.

Most variables are measured psychometrically: the proxies are based on multiple items instead of on only one (Nunnally, 1978). In this way, it is more likely that the variables are really covered by the questions (see, e.g., Agarwal and Ramaswami, 1992a; Kim and Hwang, 1992). Besides survey data, archival data were collected on, for example, host country risk, cultural distance, the level of welfare, and the level of education of the host country's inhabitants. The reason is that the combination of these two types of data allows a better measurement of variables.

4.2 Variables

The dependent variable is the mode of entry: either a JV or a WOS. Three types of JVs are distinguished: minority, 50/50, and majority JVs. In general, researchers take the division of equity as proxy for the distribution of power within a JV, mainly because this information can be acquired rather easily from public sources (see, e.g., Bell and Jagersma, 1996; Gatignon and Anderson, 1988; Gomes-Casseres, 1989). A better and more precise measure of the type of JV would be the division of control. Control is defined as the ability to influence systems, methods, decisions, and the behaviour of other parties (compare Ouchi, 1977) in order to accomplish a prespecified result. This concept is more accurate than the equity division, as partners with a 50 per cent, or even a minority, equity stake may largely control the JV (Geringer and Hebert, 1989; Schaan, 1988). In the present study, both division criteria were included. The division of equity was measured by means of a question on the percentage of equity each partner has in the JV. The control division was captured by a question on the actual influence a firm can have in the JV.

In Chapter 3, four groups of variables were found to be important in entry mode decisions: strategic variables, ownership-specific variables, transactional variables, and locational variables. In addition to these variables, three variables are distinguished to control for possible disturbing effects: the size of the investing firm, the type of industry, and the activities of the value chain performed by the foreign subsidiary. Below, the operationalization of all these variables will be explained.

Strategic variables

Global strategy: Two indicators are used to measure this variable: (1) a dummy variable which indicates whether all products of the foreign subsidiary are sold in the host country; (2) a dummy variable with the value 1 if less than 10 per cent of the sales of the foreign subsidiary is sold to the parent firm. The first indicator is included because global firms sell their products in many countries, while firms with a multi-domestic (or national responsiveness) strategy mainly sell their products locally (see Bartlett and Ghoshal, 1989; Hout, Porter, and Rudden, 1982). The second indicator provides insight into the level of intrasystem sales. Following Gomes-Casseres (1989), it is believed that if these intra-system sales are more than 10 per cent of the foreign affiliate's total sales, an important vertical relationship exists between the entry mode and the firm. Since firms with a global strategy attempt to economize on their value-chain activities by gaining economies of scale and scope, many intrafirm deliveries will take place.

Level of competition: This variable is measured by means of two indicators: (1) the respondent's perception of the intensity of the competition in the industry at the time of entry; and (2) the perceived number of (potential) competitors in the industry at the time of entry. Both indicators have a 7-point Likert scale.

Industry growth: This variable is operationalized by: (1) the respondent's perception of the present growth of the sales of the industry entered; and (2) his or her expectation of the prospects of that growth in the near future. Both indicators have a 7-point Likert-type scale. These questions are comparable with the questions used by Kim and Hwang (1992). Hennart (1991) and Kogut and Singh (1988b) took the annual rate of the growth of the shipments in the industry as the proxy for industry growth.

Ownership-specific variables

International experience: This variable is measured by: (1) the perceived multinational experience of the firm scored on a 7-point scale (compare Agarwal and Ramaswami, 1992a); (2) the number of foreign JVs and WOSs of the firm (the respondent had to select one out of five possible categories) (see, e.g., Benito, 1996; Gatignon and Anderson, 1988; Larimo, 1993); and (3) the year in which the firm established its first foreign JV or WOS (four periods were given as answering categories) (compare Erramilli, 1991; Padmanabhan and Cho, 1994). As has been demonstrated frequently, the experience curve and the learning curve are characterized by the fact that the marginal increase in experience and learning becomes smaller and smaller (see, e.g., Johnson and Scholes, 1989; Porter, 1980). Therefore, the natural logarithm of this variable was used since a logarithmic curve reflects decreasing marginal effects (compare Barkema, Bell, and Pennings, 1996).

Host country experience: In line with Kim and Hwang (1992), host experience is measured by (1) the perceived familiarity of the firm with the host country (e.g., customers' preferences, market structure, national culture); and (2) the perceived experience of the firm in operating in that country. Both indicators were scored on a 7-point scale. Again, the natural logarithm was taken.

Mode experience: This variable is measured by asking the respondent whether the firm had established at least one JV or WOS previously (compare Madhok, 1994). To capture the separate effects of JV experience and WOS experience, two dummies were created.

Product experience: Product experience is assessed by taking the difference between the core business of the subsidiary and the firm as perceived by the respondent. This difference was indicated on a 7-point scale. Product experience is closely related to the direction of expansion. In case a firm had no previous experience with a product, the expansion was labelled an unrelated diversification, and much product experience was called a horizontal expansion.

In addition to this indicator, it was attempted to determine the direction of expansion by comparing the classification codes of the core activities of both the MNE and the subsidiary (see Gomes-Casseres, 1989; Hennart, 1990; Pennings, Barkema, and Douma, 1994). The comparison resulted in only three related diversifications and no unrelated diversifications. This means that virtually all expansions fell within the core business of the investing firm. As a consequence, this classification is inappropriate for inclusion in the analyses.

Relative size: A 7-point scale was used to gain insight into the respondent's judgment of the size (measured by invested capital) of the entry mode relative to the firm (compare Hennart, 1991; Kogut and Singh, 1988b; Larimo, 1993).

Transactional variables

Asset specificity: This variable is measured by four indicators with a 7-point Likert scale: (1) the perceived degree of specific technological know-how the firm contributed to the new venture; (2) the estimated degree of proprietary skills that the firm transferred to the entry mode. These two proxies cover the level of specificity of the assets contributed. These proxies are comparable to the questions included in other empirical studies that employ survey data (see Agarwal and Ramaswami, 1992a; Erramilli and Rao, 1993; Kim and Hwang, 1992; Madhok, 1994). Studies solely based on archival data usually take the ratio of the firm's R&D expenditures and sales, or the ratio of the average R&D expenditures of the industry and the average sales of the industry, as the indicator for asset specificity (see, e.g., Caves and Mehra, 1986; Gatignon and Anderson, 1988; Hennart, 1991).

Besides these two indicators of the level of asset specificity, two questions were included on the perceived risk that other firms might exploit or even abuse the proprietary know-how and/or skills: (3) the perceived risk of opportunistic behaviour regarding the specific know-how; and (4) the perceived risk of opportunistic behaviour regarding the specific skills. These indicators were added to operationalize the crucial assumption of transaction cost economics that asset specificity and opportunism must occur simultaneously to make a WOS the most efficient governance structure (Williamson, 1975, 1985). In the absence of opportunistic behaviour, transactions characterized by asset specificity can also be governed efficiently with a partially controlled structure, such as a JV or a long-term contract.

In order to capture this combination of asset specificity and opportunism, a dummy variable was created with the value 1 if both asset specificity *and* the likelihood of opportunism are high (i.e., above the mean).[1] In all other possible situations, the dummy has the value 0.

Reputation: The investing firm's reputation is assessed by four indicators: (1) the respondent's perception of the firm's reputation in the host country before the establishment of the entry mode; (2) the respondent's perception of the firm's reputation in the industry entered in the host country; (3) the respondent's judgment of customers' assessment of the firm in comparison with competitors; and (4) the perceived investments in the firm's image relative to competitors. All four indicators were scored on a 7-point scale. The first three indicators are similar to Kim and Hwang's (1992) indicators. This method of using the respondent's perception measures a firm's reputation more directly than by using the marketing intensity of the firm or the industry as a proxy for reputation, as was done in earlier studies (compare Gatignon and Anderson, 1988; Gomes-Casseres, 1989; Hennart, 1991).

Locational variables

Cultural difference: Most previous empirical studies measured the cultural differences between the home country and the host country with either the country clusters created by Ronen and Shenkar (1985) (see, e.g., Gatignon and Anderson, 1988) or the Kogut and Singh index (see, for instance, Agarwal, 1994; Benito and Gripsrud, 1992; Cho and Padmanabhan, 1995; Errarnilli, 1991; Errarnilli and Rao, 1993; Kogut and Singh, 1988a; Larimo, 1993; Padmanabhan and Cho, 1994) or both (Barkema, Bell, and Pennings, 1996). Brouthers et al. (1993) and Kim and Hwang (1992) used questionnaires to measure perceived cultural differences. The Ronen and Shenkar (1985) clustering is based on eight cross-cultural studies, among which the frequently cited large-scale study by Hofstede (1980). The Kogut and Singh index is based on Hofstede's four dimensions of national culture: uncertainty avoidance, individualism, power distance, and masculinity. Kogut and Singh (1988a) calculated their index by subtracting the scores of the home country on each of the four dimensions from those of the host country. The square of this difference was divided by the variance of the scores on each dimension. For each host country, the resulting scores on each dimension were added up and divided by four.

In the present study, cultural difference is measured by two indicators: (1) the Kogut and Singh index; and (2) the respondent's perception (on a 7-point scale) of the cultural differences between the Netherlands and the host country. The reason for combining these indicators is that both may capture different aspects of the 'true' cultural distance.

For some of the host countries in this study, there were no scores on the cultural dimensions available (see Hofstede, 1980, 1991). These countries are China, Hungary, Poland, the Czech Republic, Estonia, Romania, Malta, Namibia, Syria, and the Netherlands Antilles. These scores were obtained from personal communication with Hofstede:

1   The scores of Hong Kong were used for China, since, nowadays, China is comparable to Hong Kong. Capitalistic principles are officially denied in China, but they flourish in practice.
2   The scores for Hungary were taken from a study by Varga (1986).
3   The scores for Poland, the Czech Republic, and Romania are estimates by Hofstede based on the characteristics of the countries.

Romania, for instance, has a Byzantine background which heavily influenced its scores on the four cultural dimensions.

4   The scores for Finland were used for Estonia, since the countries are comparable. One exception, however, is the dimension of individualism, for which Hofstede suggested a lower score.
5   Namibia can be considered to be a West African country. Therefore, the scores for West Africa were also used for Namibia.
6   Syria can be considered to be a Arab country. Therefore, the scores for the Arab region were used for Syria.
7   There are no data on the Netherlands Antilles, therefore the scores for Surinam were used. The reason is that this country, mainly because of its close relationship with the Netherlands, appears to be similar to the Netherlands Antilles. The scores for Surinam were taken from the study by Nanhekhan (1990).

Hofstede was not able to provide the scores for Malta. He referred to M. Hoppe, who replicated Hofstede's study for nineteen countries including Malta (see Hoppe, 1990). In a personal communication with Hoppe, these missing scores were obtained. According to Hoppe, Malta is comparable to the Latin European countries.

As was shown in Chapter 3, cultural distance is hypothesized to have a curve-linear, U-shaped effect on the incidence of JVs. In order to test this relationship, the square of the variable cultural distance was also included in the model.

Host country risk: In previous studies, host country risk was frequently captured by the classification made by Goodnow and Hanz (1972) (see Benito, 1996; Erramilli and Rao, 1993; Gatignon and Anderson, 1988). A disadvantage of this classification is that it gives an impression of the risk of countries in the late 1960s. This classification may no longer hold, especially because the riskiness of countries varies over time. For example, countries such as India, Thailand, and Turkey, which were high-risk countries according to Goodnow and Hanz, are less risky nowadays. Agarwal (1994) and Agarwal and Ramaswami (1992a, 1992b) took more recent data from the annually published International Country Risk Guide. Instead of using these 'objective' measures of country risk, Kim and Hwang (1992) based country risk on the respondents' perceptions.

In this study, the two methods are combined: the perceptions of respondents are complemented with publicly available data on country risk. This combination was done for reasons similar to those in the case of cultural differences (see above). The riskiness of the host country was measured by: (1) the perceived political stability in the host country; (2) the perceived economic situation of the host country; (3) the perceived risks of the host country other than political and economic risks (e.g., the risks of natural disasters); and (4) the country risk score in the year of entry as calculated by Euromoney. The first three indicators are the respondents' judgments (on a 7-point scale) about the riskiness of the host country in the period of the establishment of the foreign subsidiary. The fourth indicator was taken from the rankings of country risk published annually by Euromoney.

Once a year, and since recently twice a year, Euromoney publishes a list of the riskiness of all countries in the world. This country risk score consists of three broad categories: (a) analytical indicators (political risk, economic risk, and economic indicators); (b) credit indicators (payment record and ease of rescheduling); and (c) market indicators (access to short-term and long-term finance). Each category has a different weighting factor, with economic risk and political risk having the greatest weight. Euromoney uses data from several sources, such as the World Bank World Debt Tables, the Euromoney global economic projections, and expert polls to calculate the host country risk. Experts from all over the world (risk analysts, risk insurance brokers, and bank credit officers) are polled to obtain estimates of the political risks.

Host government policy: Several previous studies included this variable in their analyses. For instance, Gatignon and Anderson (1988) used the classification by Stopford and Wells (1972), who distinguished six restrictive countries. Gomes-Casseres (1989, 1990) created a dummy variable with the value 1 for countries which had restricted foreign ownership or had encouraged JVs in 1975. Gomes-Casseres used data from the US Department of Commerce. A shortcoming of these measures is that they disregard the fact that countries may change their attitudes and their policies towards foreign investments. Illustrative in this regard is the strong relaxation of restrictive policies which has taken place in the 1980s (see, e.g., Contractor, 1990b). A better approach is to look at government policy at the moment (or year) of entry (compare Padmanabhan and Cho, 1994); in that case, the influence of the host government on the entry mode choice can be adequately assessed. A different method was employed by Kim and Hwang (1992). They asked managers how they perceived the likelihood that the host government would put constraints on foreign operations.

In the present study, the perceptions of the respondents are combined with a more 'objective' measure of the government policy in the year of entry. The reason is that restrictions may affect investing firms differently, since some firms may have enough bargaining power to minimize the impact of governmental restrictions.[2] Hence, the (perceived) impact on the individual firms should not be ignored. Therefore, the following indicators were used to determine the policies of host governments: (1) the managers' perception (on a 7-point scale) of the restrictiveness of the host government with regard to the firm's investment; (2) the respondents' perception (on a 7-point scale) of the extent to which the host government stimulated cooperation with local firms; and (3) data on the restrictiveness of host governments in the year of entry which were gathered from publications by the Dutch Ministry of Economic Affairs, the IMF, the OECD, the UNCTC, and the World Bank. A dummy variable captured whether a host country was restrictive (value 1) or not (value 0) in the year of entry.

More specifically, the following countries were classified as restrictive: China, Indonesia, India, Japan, Poland, Romania, Saudi Arabia, Syria, Thailand, and Turkey. This list of countries is comparable to the results which Contractor (1990b) found using the Benchmark Surveys. Some countries use more restrictions than others. Indonesia, India, and Romania, for instance, heavily restricted foreign ownership for all industries, whereas other countries (e.g., Japan) only limited foreign ownership in specific industries.

Level of welfare: In earlier studies, the level of welfare in the host country was assessed by taking the Gross Domestic Product (GDP) of countries (Gomes-Casseres, 1989, 1990; Larimo, 1993; Shane, 1993) or the Gross Net Product (GNP) per capita (Agarwal, 1994; Benito, 1996). In the present study, the latter indicator is preferred since it provides more insight into the welfare of individual customers. A heavily populated country with a high GDP may still have a low level of welfare.

In addition to (1) the GNP per capita (in US dollars), the level of welfare is measured by four other proxies: (2) the secondary school enrolment ratio; (3) the third school enrolment ratio (i.e., the number of students per 100,000 inhabitants); (4) the percentage of illiterates; and (5) the respondent's perception (on a 7-point scale) of the attractiveness of the local firms' level of knowledge and level of education. If available, data on these indicators were collected for the year of entry. Alternatively, the nearest year was taken, which was never more than three years removed from the year of entry. The GNP per capita was taken from the World Tables 1992 (World Bank, 1993). Data on the secondary school enrolment ratio were also collected from the World Tables, and the third school enrolment ratio was taken from the Unesco Statistical Yearbooks. The illiteracy rates were also obtained from these Yearbooks and the Compendium of Statistics on Illiteracy (Unesco, 1990).

Control variables

Three variables are included as control variables: the size of the investing firm, the type of industry it is involved in, and the type of activity of the foreign affiliate.

Firm size: The size of the expanding firm may affect the entry mode choice. Larger firms have more resources than smaller firms. Therefore, they are less inclined to set up JVs than smaller firms for reasons of managerial and financial constraints. In line with previous studies (e.g., Agarwal and Ramaswami, 1992a; Benito, 1996; Larimo, 1993), the sales of the investing firm is used as a proxy for the size of the investing firm. Respondents were asked to give information about sales over 1992 of their firm, division or business unit, depending on their position. If no information was provided on firm sales, annual reports were consulted to try to obtain these data. A logarithmic function of the 1992 sales was used (compare Barkema, Bell, and Pennings, 1996; Padmanabhan and Cho, 1994).

Type of industry: Previous studies found that in certain industries firms prefer full ownership over shared ownership, e.g., in advertising-intensive industries, and know-how-intensive industries (Franko, 1989; Gomes-Casseres, 1989). Alternatively, firms prefer JVs over WOSs in resource-intensive industries (Gomes-Casseres, 1989; Harrigan, 1985a; Hennart, 1991; Larimo, 1993). To determine whether an industry is advertising intensive or know-how intensive usually the average marketing-to-sales ratio and the R&D-to-sales ratio of the industry, respectively, are used (see, e.g., Gomes-Casseres, 1989; Kogut and Singh, 198-8b). Industries are called resource intensive if their main products involve food and beverages, tobacco, textile mills, wood (except furniture), pulp and paper, petroleum, rubber, and primary metals (see Gomes-Casseres, 1989).

In the present study, the respondents were asked to indicate the core product of the new subsidiary. This information was used to ascertain which industry was entered. The determination of resource-intensive industries was done with the help of Gomes-Casseres's classification. In the Netherlands, no data are available on the marketing-to-sales and R&D-to-sales ratios. Furthermore, no classifications of more know-how-intensive and marketing-intensive industries exist. As a consequence, own classifications were made. Industries were classified as know-how intensive or marketing intensive if in the particular industry, many financial resources were expected to be devoted to R&D or to marketing. In addition, it was checked which industries have earlier been labelled as know-how intensive or marketing intensive in the literature (see, e.g., Brickley and Dark, 1987; Cohen and Levin, 1989; Franko, 1989; Harrigan, 1985a; Schmalensee, 1989; Stopford and Wells, 1972). Some of the industries which have been labelled as know-how intensive are: electronics, coatings, optical instruments, and fibres. Advertising-intensive industries are consumer food, clothing, pharmaceuticals, and so on.

Type of activity: The foreign subsidiary's type of activities may be crucial for the decision concerning the appropriate entry mode (see Bell and Jagersma, 1996). If the affiliate's main activity involves marketing and sales, it is to be expected that a firm wants to control this vital link of the value chain alone (Porter, 1986; Porter and Fuller, 1986). Full control enables the firm to ensure a good quality of the sales trajectory and a high commitment of the sales people. Furthermore, it prevents a deterioration of the firm's brand name and image (see, e.g., Anderson and Gatignon, 1986; Brickley and Dark, 1987).

Similarly, firms may prefer to control the production of goods, for instance, to prevent deterioration of the quality of the production process and of the final products. This preference will be especially strong if the production process is complex and requires much tacit knowledge to proceed smoothly (Teece, 1976; Williamson, 1979). Rather simple production processes and mature products do not necessitate high control, because the requisite knowledge is widely available and relatively easy to manage (Anderson and Gatignon, 1986; Teece, 1976).

Finally, JVs may be advantageous in situations of (technological) know-how development, since the knowledge base of more firms can be combined and exchanged to achieve positive synergies (see, e.g., Contractor, 1990a; Contractor and Lorange, 1988b; Harrigan, 1985a). However, it can be argued that such new, advanced know-how should not be shared with other firms to prevent the other firm from taking away the know-how and from using it exclusively for its own benefits (Hamel, 1991; Hamel, Doz, and Prahalad, 1989; Reich and Mankin, 1986). The choice between a JV and a WOS depends on the relationship with a partner firm and the possibilities of preventing opportunistic behaviour.

The foreign subsidiary's type of activity is assessed in the survey by one question that distinguishes among three possible activities: R&D, production, and marketing and sales. The respondents were asked to indicate which activity, or combination of activities, was executed in the new subsidiary.

Most variables were assessed by composite measures, which has far-reaching consequences for which statistical techniques can be applied (see section 4.4). Before examining these techniques, the sample will be described.

4.3 Sample

Important steps in the process of data collection are selecting the respondents and ensuring their participation in the survey. A description of these steps will be given below.

Unfortunately, there are no listings or databases available which contain all Dutch firms that are actively involved in foreign countries with a JV or a WOS, *and* are able to decide upon foreign entries. Firms which do not have the decision-making power to make foreign entries, such as daughter firms of foreign companies, should not enter the dataset. The entry mode choice of these firms is probably not based on the four groups of variables, but on headquarters' preferences. Fortunately, a database containing some basic data (e.g., name, address, telephone number) of the largest firms in the Netherlands could be used. This database, however, was built for a different purpose. Hence, it is unlikely that all the firms included have a foreign JV or WOS, and have the authority to establish foreign entries. The database was constructed by including firms that appeared at least once in any of the following rankings:

1   the *FEM* top 100 of 1990 and 1991 based on net value added;[3]
2   the *FD* top 50 of 1992 based on net profits;
3   the *FD* top 50 of 1992 based on cash flows;
4   the *FD* top 50 of 1992 based on total assets;
5   the *FD* top 50 of 1992 based on shareholders' value;
6   the *FD* top 50 of 1992 based on the number of employees;
7   the *FD* top 100 of 1992 based on sales.[4]

This procedure led to a database of exactly 250 large Dutch firms. Also, several divisions and business units of these firms were added to the database. The reason is that exploratory interviews revealed that in many large firms not only headquarters decide upon foreign entries and mode choices, but also the divisions, and even (large) business units.[5] Hence, the 1992 annual reports of these 250 firms were examined to discover possible international involvement of divisions and business units. In all cases where the list of participations - which is included in Dutch annual reports - contained one or more foreign affiliates, the particular division or business unit was incorporated in the database. This method resulted in 139 extra observations.

Furthermore, it was attempted to find other internationalized firms, which were not among the 250 biggest Dutch firms. For this purpose, *het Financieel Economisch Lexicon* (*Financial Economic Lexicon*) of 1992 was checked, which contains an overview of Dutch firms and their subsidiaries and participations. This examination revealed 69 additional firms which are actively involved in foreign countries.

The three trajectories combined resulted in a database of 458 firms. There is no evidence that all Dutch firms with a foreign JV or WOS are incorporated in this database, or that all included firms actually have a foreign JV or WOS. Moreover, it is not clear whether all firms, divisions, and business units can decide upon the entry mode when they enter a foreign country. The firms were phoned to establish whether they possessed foreign JVs or WOSs, and to establish their autonomy in foreign entry mode decisions.

In an attempt to ensure a high level of participation and a high response rate, the following actions were taken:

1 The Secretary of the Executive Board[6] of each firm was called to ask for the name and telephone number of the most appropriate respondent for this study. This should be a person who was closely involved in one or more recent foreign entries, for example, a member of the Executive Board, the CEO, a strategic planner, the director geographic development, or the head of the international division. At the level of the division and the business unit, the head or the strategic planner are the most appropriate respondents. In most cases, the secretaries were able to refer to the right persons. Occasionally, they proposed to address the questionnaire to them so that they could see to it that the questionnaire would be filled in by the appropriate person.
2 The potential respondents were approached by telephone to find out whether they would be willing to participate in the survey. In this way, further information could be provided orally. An additional advantage is that respondents tend to remember the phonecall when they receive the questionnaire, which may have a positive effect on his or her willingness to fill it in.
3 As an extra stimulus to complete the questionnaire, the potential respondents were promised a report with the results of the study. Furthermore, they received an invitation to a (free) workshop about

the results of the study.
4 The questionnaire itself was set up in such a way that it could be filled in easily within a limited amount of time. Moreover, much attention was paid to making a well-structured layout (see Appendix A). Of course, it was stressed that the data would be dealt with confidentially, and that anonymity was assured. With regard to the contents of the questionnaire, two distinct tests were carried out. First, during the construction of the survey, a number of experts (both in international management and in survey methodology) checked both the translation of theoretical concepts into specific questions, and the formulation of the questions. Second, two potential respondents scrutinized the questionnaire. They were asked to think aloud while interpreting and answering the questions. This testing stage provided some insight into the interpretation of the questions. On the whole, the questions were understood in the way that they were meant, but a few adjustments in the formulation of questions proved to be necessary.
5 After some weeks, a reminder was sent to the firms that had not yet returned the questionnaire.

In order to obtain the information required for the empirical analyses, it is a prerequisite that the respondents are well informed about the decision process preceding the choice of the mode of foreign entry. The respondents were asked to remember a recently established foreign JV and/or WOS in which they themselves were involved. Subsequently, they had to answer the questions. If a respondent had been involved in both types of entry, he/she was asked to fill in the questions for both.

All but 28 of the total group of 458 firms were phoned to find out whether the firm would participate in the survey. The reasons for not contacting the 28 firms were, for example, the inability to trace address or telephone number and the reluctance to call firms whose survival was at stake at that time. Of the remaining 430 firms, 127 firms did not participate for several reasons: 80 firms indicated that they had no foreign JV or WOS; 19 firms were fully owned by foreign firms and had no decision power regarding foreign entry mode choices; and 28 firms stated that they did not want to cooperate in the survey, because of a shortage of time and the confidentiality of the information.

As a result, 303 questionnaires were distributed by mail. Of the 303 questionnaires, 164 were returned, which is a response rate of 54 per cent. This response rate is much higher than in previous entry mode studies, where a response rate of 20-25 per cent is normal (see Agarwal and Ramaswami, 1992a; Brouthers et al., 1993; Kim and Hwang, 1992;

Madhok, 1994). Only in some studies, a higher response rate was obtained (Erramilli, 1991: 44 per cent; Larimo, 1993: 30 per cent).

Of the 164 questionnaires returned, 46 were not filled in because the firms did not have a foreign JV or WOS (18) or the firms did not want to participate (28). Careful examination of the returned questionnaires revealed that four more could not be used, which resulted in 114 usable questionnaires. The respondents were asked to fill in the questions for either a JV or a WOS or for both. A number of them completed the questionnaire for both a JV and a WOS, which finally resulted in 168 usable observations (75 JVs and 93 WOSs). A list of the host countries entered is included in Appendix B.

This section described the sample. In the next section, the statistical techniques that were used to test the hypotheses will be explained.

4.4 Statistical techniques

As indicated in section 4.2, most independent variables are proxied by more than one indicator. To find out whether these items measure the same underlying variable, confirmatory factor analysis was used (compare Frambach, 1993; Long, 1983a). This technique tests whether a number of observed indicators together measure an unobservable underlying variable. The relationships among those underlying variables cannot be tested with confirmatory factor analysis. In the present study, these relationships were tested with logit models.

By separating the measurement model and the testing model, a so-called two-step approach was followed (Anderson and Gerbing, 1988). An alternative would be a structural equation model in which both distinct steps are taken simultaneously (see, e.g., Bollen, 1989; Byrne, 1989; Lim, Sharkey, and Kim, 1991; Long, 1983b). This one-step approach, however, has a number of shortcomings (see, e.g., Anderson and Gerbing, 1988, 1992). First, incorrect specifications influence all estimates (Johnston, 1984). Second, it is almost inevitable that interpretational confounding will take place. Interpretational confounding means that an unobserved variable is given a different empirical meaning than would have been given by an individual before estimating unknown parameters (Burt, 1973). This effect is reflected by the substantial changes in the parameter estimates when different structural models are tested. It is caused by the fact that the covariances of indicators, which are not related according to the theoretical specification, affect the estimations and the fit of the model. A two-step approach prevents these problems with incorrect specification and interpretational confounding.

The two-step approach has drawbacks as well (see, e.g., Fornell and Yi, 1992). One limitation is that the two steps are not completely independent, as is suggested by the label 'two-step approach': modifications in the first stage affect the second stage. In a reaction to this criticism, Anderson and Gerbing (1992) argued that the specification and its modifications in the first stage are based on theory, which implies that possible effects on the second stage are not arbitrary but driven by theory.

The second step, i.e., testing the relationships among the independent variables and between the independent variables and the dependent variable, was done with logit analysis.[7] 'Normal' (multiple) regression techniques (e.g., OLS) cannot be used, as the dependent variable is not a continuous variable. Hence, qualitative response models (Amemiya, 1981), which acknowledge the discrete nature of the dependent variable, should be used. Three different models will be described. First, if the dependent variable is dichotomous (JV versus WOS), an appropriate statistical technique is a binomial logit model (DeMaris, 1992). Second, if the dependent variable can take more than two discrete values (minority JV, 50/50 JV, majority JV, and WOS), a multinomial logit model is appropriate (DeMaris, 1992; Liao, 1994; Menard, 1995). Third, if the values of the dependent variable are ordered, as is suggested in foreign entry mode literature (e.g., Chu and Anderson, 1992; Contractor and Lorange, 1988b; Hagedoorn, 1993; Root, 1987), an ordered logit model is suitable (DeMaris, 1992; Ishii-Kuntz, 1994).

Confirmatory factor analysis

Confirmatory factor analysis is used for measuring the effects of indicators on latent or underlying variables. Indicators which are believed to operationalize the same construct are combined into one model. Then, the analysis is directed at examining whether the empirical data can confirm the theoretical model specified ex ante.

The confirmatory factor analytic model can be written as (see, e.g., Bollen, 1989; Byrne, 1989; Long, 1983a):

$$x = \Lambda_x \xi + \delta \qquad [4.1]$$

where x is a (qx1) vector of indicators or observed variables; Λ_x is a (qxs) matrix of factor loadings relating the x's to the latent ξ's; ξ is an (sx1) vector of constructs or latent variables; and δ is a (qx1) vector of the unique factors or measurement errors.

Figure 4.1 contains an example of a schematic presentation of a confirmatory factor analytic model. In this figure, it is shown that latent variables (ξ_j's) may be correlated. Although not depicted in this figure, the measurement errors (δ_i's) can be related too.

Confirmatory factor analysis needs a correlation matrix or a covariance matrix of the observed variables as input matrix. The covariance matrix should be used as the input matrix if all variables are continuous variables, because it prevents a loss of valuable information on the dispersion of variables (Jöreskog and Sörbom, 1988). However, if at least some variables have a discrete nature (either ordinal or nominal), the correlation matrix will be the most appropriate input matrix. In that case, the variances of the variables cannot be calculated since the central tendency is unknown (Churchill, 1991). Contingent on the measurement scale of the observed variables (nominal, ordinal, interval, or ratio), a different type of correlation coefficient is applicable. A polychorical correlation coefficient is calculated in case there are two ordinal variables. In the case of one ordinal variable and one continuous variable, a polyserial correlation coefficient is computed. Finally, a Pearson correlation matrix is calculated if both variables are continuous (Jöreskog and Sörbom, 1988).

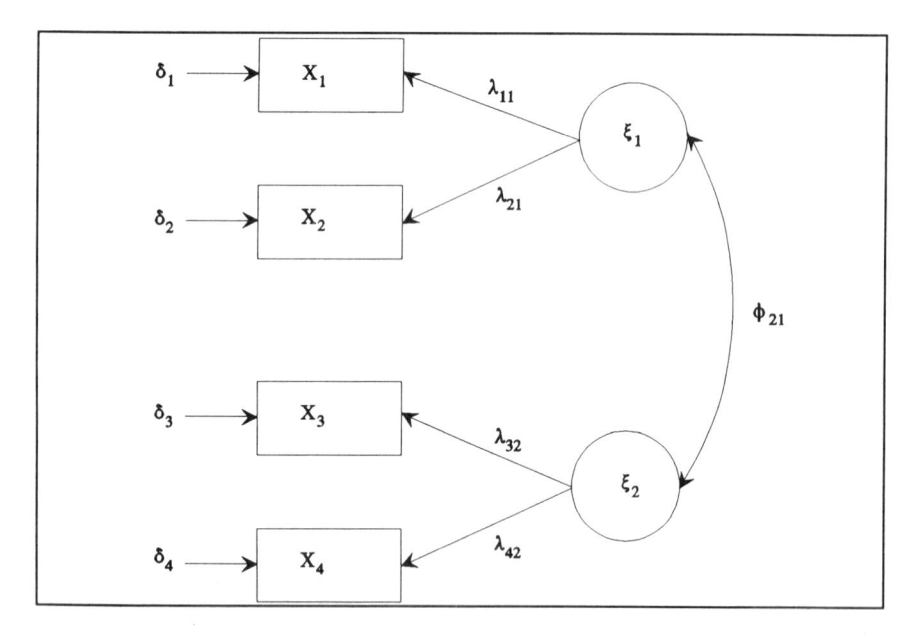

Figure 4.1 Confirmatory factor analytic model

In the present study, the measurement scale of the observed variables ranges from ordinal to ratio. As a result, a covariance matrix cannot be used as the input matrix. PRELIS was used to calculate the correlation matrices, as it has an option with which the cut-off rate can be specified when a variable is interpreted as an ordinal variable or as an interval variable (Jöreskog and Sörbom, 1988). The confirmatory factor analyses were carried out using LISREL's maximum likelihood procedure (Jöreskog and Sörbom, 1989), which is common practice for this purpose (Bollen, 1989). This technique produces the best estimations if the variables have a normal distribution. Based on the rule of thumb that the kurtosis and skewness should not exceed $|1|$ (Churchill, 1991), it turned out that most independent variables are more or less normally distributed. Nevertheless, the outcomes should be interpreted with care. If not all variables have a normal distribution, maximum likelihood may estimate the standard errors and the χ^2 goodness-of-fit measures incorrectly (Cudeck, 1989). In the present study, these limitations are mitigated by requiring that the t-values must exceed the value 2 before they are interpreted as significant (see Boomsma, 1983). Moreover, χ^2 will not be used to examine the goodness-of-fit of the theoretical matrix and the empirical matrix.

Other measures for the model fit, such as the adjusted goodness-of-fit index (AGFI) and the root mean squared residual (RMR), are more appropriate in the present context (Jöreskog and Sörbom, 1989). The AGFI indicates how much of the covariance is explained by the model parameters, taking into account the number of degrees of freedom. The value of the AGFI can range from 0 to 1, where a higher value means that the fit is better. The RMR measures the average of the variance of the residuals that cannot be explained by the model. The RMR has the same range as the AGFI, but here a value closer to 0 implies a better fit.

In addition to these measures of the overall fit of the models, it is also possible to evaluate the estimates of the individual indicators. Four important measures will be used: validity, reliability, the coefficient of determination, and the largest fitted residual. First, validity involves the question whether a variable measures what it is supposed to measure (Churchill, 1991; Cook and Campbell, 1979). In confirmatory factor analytic models, the (convergent) validity of an indicator is the λ_{ij}, i.e., the size of the direct relationship between one latent variable and one indicator (Anderson and Gerbing, 1988; Bollen, 1989). Whether indicator x_i measures what it is supposed to do, is signalled by the significance of λ_{ij}. As mentioned above, the threshold for significance employed in this study is that the t-value must be at least 2. The validity of a construct can be calculated as follows: $\Sigma\lambda_i^2/(\Sigma\lambda_i^2+\Sigma\delta_i)$.

Second, reliability means that the same results will be obtained when the same procedures or tests will be done again with the same data (Yin, 1989). In LISREL, the reliability of an indicator is defined as the direct relationship between all latent variables and indicator x_i (Bollen, 1989). The larger this direct relationship, the larger the reliability of x_i. The reliability is measured with R^2 (i.e., the squared multiple correlation coefficient of x_i), which can range from 0 to 1. Since, in this study, each indicator is influenced by only one latent variable, the R^2 is equal to λ^2. The reliability of a latent variable can be computed with the formula: $(\Sigma\lambda_i)^2/((\Sigma\lambda_i)^2 + \Sigma\delta_i)$.

Third, the coefficient of determination indicates how well the indicators jointly measure the latent variable (Jöreskog and Sörbom, 1989). A higher value (i.e., closer to 1) means that the model is better. The fourth measure examines the residuals, which consist of the difference between the theoretical and the empirical correlation matrices. A model is called a good model if the value of the largest fitted residual is smaller than 0.1 (Backhaus et al., 1987).

So far, only the relationships between the latent variable and the individual indicators were discussed. LISREL provides so-called 'factor score regressions', which are regression coefficients between the indicators and all latent variables. These 'factor score regressions' were multiplied by the respondents' scores on the various indicators, resulting in the respondents' scores on the latent variables.[8]

In this section, the main elements of the first step of the two-step model were discussed. Below, the second step, i.e., the testing of the relationships between, on the one hand, the choice of entry mode, and, on the other hand, the various latent variables will be discussed.

Binomial logit analysis

Binomial logit models have been used frequently in foreign entry mode studies (see e.g., Cho and Padmanabhan, 1995; Davidson and McFetridge, 1985; Gatignon and Anderson, 1988; Gomes-Casseres, 1989; Hennart, 1991; Larimo, 1993). Binomial logit analysis is oriented to estimating the probability that an event occurs rather than another. In the present study, it would mean that instead of a JV a WOS is chosen as the foreign entry mode. The binomial logit model can be formalized as follows (Norušis, 1990):

$$P(Y) = \frac{e^Z}{1+e^Z} \qquad [4.2]$$

with Z being a linear combination of the independent variables:

$$Z = \beta_0 + \beta_1 X_1 + \beta_2 X_2 + \ldots + \beta_n X_n \qquad [4.3]$$

where Y is the selection of a JV as the mode of foreign entry; the β_k's are the regression coefficients, with k = 0, 1, ..., n; the X_i's are the independent variables, with i = 1, 2, ..., n. The choice for a WOS is represented by (1-Y). A positive sign for a regression coefficient means that the particular variable increases the likelihood of a JV as the selected entry mode.

If the model is written in terms of the log odds (= the logit), the direct impact of the β_k's can be shown.

$$\log \frac{P(Y)}{1 - P(Y)} = \beta_0 + \beta_1 X_1 + \beta_2 X_2 + \ldots + \beta_n X_n \qquad [4.4]$$

Logit models were estimated with SPSS 5.0 using maximum likelihood. This technique selects those β_k's that make the observed results most likely (see Cramer, 1991). Several measures exist to evaluate how well an estimated model fits the data. First, a classification table can be calculated to compare the predicted JVs and WOSs to the observed ones. A model is said to clas- sify well if the total percentage of correct predictions is substantially higher than the percentage that would have been obtained by chance. The classification rate of a random model is $\alpha^2 + (1-\alpha)^2$, where α is the proportion of JVs in the sample (see Morrison, 1969). The classification table also displays the sensitivity rate and the specificity rate of the model. The sensitivity rate indicates the ability of a model to correctly classify the dependent variable with a value of 1 (JVs), whereas the specificity rate indicates the opposite.

A second way of assessing goodness of fit is to investigate the likelihood of the sample outcomes, given the estimates of the parameters. A common measure is the -2 times the log likelihood (-2LL), which has a small value if the fit is well. This measure can be used to test whether the predicted model is comparable to the perfect model. An insignificant result indicates that the null hypothesis - that the models resemble each other - cannot be rejected.

A third way to determine goodness of fit is the model-χ^2, which tests the null hypothesis that all β_k's are zero, except β_0. Whenever the model-χ^2 is significant, this null hypothesis can be rejected.

The binomial logit model is only applicable if the dependent variable is a dichotomous variable. Sometimes, the dependent variable may take more than two values. In this study, three different types of JVs were distinguished: majority, 50/50, and minority JVs. Firms entering a foreign market may opt for either a WOS or one of the three types of JVs; a choice out of four possible entry modes. Then, multinomial rather than binomial logit analysis can be used to estimate the effects of the independent variables on the entry mode choice. This technique will be discussed in the next subsection.

Multinomial logit analysis

Multinomial logit analysis can be applied if the dependent variable has at least three categories that need not be ordered. Many empirical studies on foreign entry mode choices used multinomial logit analysis (see, e.g., Agarwal and Ramaswami, 1992a; Contractor, 1984; Erramilli, 1991; Gatignon and Anderson, 1988; Kim and Hwang, 1992; Kogut and Singh, 1988a).

Multinomial logit analysis is directed at estimating the effects of independent variables on the probability that a certain state of an event occurs. Formally (Liao, 1994):

$$P(Y=j) = \frac{e^{W_j}}{1 + \sum_{j=1}^{J-1} e^{W_j}} \qquad [4.5]$$

with W being a linear combination of the independent variables

$$W_j = \beta_{j0} + \beta_{j1} X_1 + \beta_{j2} X_2 + ... + \beta_{jn} X_n \qquad [4.6]$$

where j represents the categories of the dependent variable, with j = 1, 2, ..., J-1; the β_k's are the regression coefficients, with k = 0, 1, ..., n; the X_i's are the independent variables, with i = 1, 2, ..., n. Response category J, P(Y=J), is the reference category, which is used as the basis for comparison. The probability that a certain response category j will be selected is the probability compared to reference category J. Obviously, this model equals the binomial logit model if J=2.

An essential condition for a correct interpretation of the outcomes of multinomial logit analysis is that the probability of a response category (e.g., a minority JV) for an individual observation is not systematically influenced by other response categories (Liao, 1994; Menard, 1995). Only if response categories are mutually exclusive and independent from one another, the precise effect of an independent variable on the incidence of a certain response category can be determined.

The goodness of fit of the multinomial logit models will be assessed in several ways (see DeMaris, 1992). First, the loglikelihood ratio test will be used. This test is an χ^2-based, global test for the significance of the total model, which is calculated as the ratio of -2LL of the model with only the intercept and the -2LL of the full model. The null hypothesis is that all β_k's are equal to zero. If the ratio is significant, this hypothesis is rejected. The second test is almost identical to the first one. The main difference is that the test is not meant for all β_k's, but only for a specific β_k which indicates the influence of a specific independent variable on the dependent variable. The third test (ρ^2) is a measure of the overall fit of the model, which is similar to R^2 in regression analysis (see Chu and Anderson, 1992). This measure is calculated as: $\rho^2 = 1 - L^F/L^0$, where L^F is the loglikelihood of the full model and L^0 is the loglikelihood of a model with all parameters restricted to zero. The multinomial logit analyses were carried out with the CATMOD procedure in SAS using maximum likelihood.

Ordered logit analysis

Unlike multinomial logit analysis, ordered response logit analysis assumes that the answer categories are of an ordinal nature. In the present study, this means that the four possible modes of foreign entry are ordered. This is a realistic assumption since the four entry modes range from low to high with regard to both the level of control and the level of equity. For example, in case of a minority JV, the investing firm has the least equity and (usually) the least control.[9] In spite of the intuitive appeal of the ordering of the dependent variable, virtually no empirical study on foreign entry mode choices has acknowledged it. One exception is the study by Chu and Anderson (1992). This is a replication of Gatignon and Anderson (1988), who used binomial and multinomial logit analysis. Chu and Anderson came to the conclusion that ordered logit analysis is an attractive technique for entry mode research, because it offers more parsimony and has less computational restrictions than multinomial logit analysis.

The ordered logit model can be formalized as follows:

$$P(Y \leq j) = \frac{e^{\mu_j - Z}}{1 + e^{\mu_j - Z}} \qquad [4.7]$$

where the μ_j's are unknown threshold parameters that separate the contiguous categories that have to be estimated with the β_k's (Liao,

1994). All other parameters have the same meaning as before.

One goodness-of-fit measure is added to those applied in multinomial logit analysis (see Chu and Anderson, 1992; DeMaris, 1992): the invariance to the cutpoint. This measure assumes that the estimated effects for each value of the independent variables are similar for all categories of the dependent variable (Menard, 1995). Whenever the test is insignificant, this assumption is accepted. The ordered logit analyses were carried out with the LOGISTIC command in SAS using maximum likelihood.

4.5 Conclusions

This chapter described the methodology used to test the hypotheses of the present study. In several respects, the methodology differs from the methodology employed in previous studies. The first difference is that latent variables are used which were measured by a number of indicators. Most other studies only took one proxy for each variable. Second, data about these indicators at the level of the firm or the venture were gathered by means of a survey, complemented with archival data. In this way, it was possible to include information on the perceptions of decision makers. Many previous studies only used archival data, usually, at industry level. Third, the sample consists of Dutch MNEs entering foreign countries, which adds to the general focus on US or Japanese MNEs. A last difference is that not only binomial or multinomial logit analyses were carried out, but also ordered logit analysis. This last technique was applied only once in foreign entry mode studies (see Chu and Anderson, 1992).

Chapter 5 contains the results of the statistical analyses that were carried out to test the hypotheses.

Notes

1 The mean value of these two constructs, 'asset specificity' and 'chance of opportunism', was calculated by taking the average of the multiplication of the respondents' scores on the indicators by the so-called 'factor score regressions'.
2 A firm's bargaining power depends on a variety of aspects including the state of technological know-how that may be transferred to the new subsidiary and the availability of substitutes (see Fagre and Wells, 1982; Gomes-Casseres, 1990; Kobrin, 1987; Lecraw, 1984).

3   FEM stands for *Financieel Economisch Magazine* (*Financial Economic Magazine*), which publishes a list of the 100 biggest Dutch firms every year.
4   FD is the abbreviation of *Het Financieele Dagblad* (*The Financial Daily*), the Dutch equivalent of *The Financial Times* and *The Wall Street Journal*. Each year a special volume is published which contains rankings of Dutch firms ordered on the basis of various criteria.
5   In case two or more questionnaires were received from one firm, it was checked whether the ventures differed. In all cases, the ventures were, indeed, different.
6   In the Netherlands, firms are managed by an Executive Board, which consists of the Chief Executive Officer (CEO) and some other top managers. In general, each top manager is responsible for a functional area, such as marketing, production, finance, or a geographical area, such as Western Europe, North America, the Far East. In contrast with most Anglo-Saxon firms, decisions are taken by the Executive Board rather than by the CEO.
7   In general, probit models produce results similar to logit models (Aldrich and Nelson, 1984; Liao, 1994). The models differ with regard to the assumed distribution of the disturbance term. Logit analysis assumes a logistic distribution function, while probit analysis assumes a normal distribution. In line with most previous studies on foreign entry modes, this study will use logit analysis.
8   These multiplications were executed with 386-MATLAB. Missing values in the indicator scores were substituted by the mean value of the scores of the remaining respondents on that particular indicator. This method, called 'mean imputation', adds noise to the model, making significant relationships less likely (Little and Rubin, 1987).
9   A minority stake in the equity of a JV does not necessarily imply that the firm has a low level of control (Schaan, 1988). Even as a minority partner, a firm can exert a substantial amount of control.

5 Results

The previous chapter focused on the methodology used to test the hypotheses as formulated in Chapter 3. The results of both steps of the two-step approach are presented in this chapter. The first step involves the estimation of the measurement model by means of confirmatory factor analysis. The results of this step are provided in section 5.2. The second step consists of testing the model. The results of the binomial, multinomial, and ordered logit analyses are discussed in sections 5.3 to 5.5, respectively. However, before these results are presented, attention will be paid to potential biases with regard to the responding firms (section 5.1).

5.1 Non-response analysis

To trace non-response bias, it was investigated whether the results obtained from the analyses are driven by differences between the group of respondents and the group of non-respondents. Non-response bias may cause inaccurate conclusions, and, consequently, reduce the external validity of a study. Several firm-related factors (e.g., firm size, the type of activity it is involved in, the type of industry) can be used to check for non-response bias. Here, the sales of the firms participating in the survey were compared to the sales of the non-responding firms. Unfortunately, it was impossible to obtain the sales of all firms, divisions, and business units included in the sample. The 1992 sales of a total of 206 non-responding and 112 responding firms could be collected.[1]

Two tests were conducted to find out whether the average firm size of the responding firms differed significantly from that of the non-responding firms. First, a T-test was done to explore whether the group means differ from each other. The null hypothesis that the group means are equal could not be rejected: the T-test is highly insignificant (p=0.94). The mean of the 1992 sales (in guilders) of the responding firms is 2,458,386 and the non-responding firms' average sales are 2,382,726. As a second test, a binomial logit model was estimated to test the effect of the firms' sales in 1992 on the decision to participate in the survey or not. The results of this logit model show that the 1992 sales have no effect at all on the firms' participation in the survey (β=9.04E-10; p=0.9435). The improvement of the model with the sales relative to the base model with only the intercept is highly insignificant (p=0.9437). This indicates that sales are not a significant predictor of survey participation. The conclusion on the basis of both tests is that the two groups of firms do not differ in size.

5.2 Confirmatory factor analysis

This section contains a discussion of the results of the first step of the two-step approach: the estimation of the measurement model. The control variables and three explanatory variables (i.e., relative size, mode experience, and product experience) are each measured by one single indicator. These variables do not have to be estimated by way of confirmatory factor analysis (CFA), but can directly be inserted in the logit analyses. All other explanatory variables are latent variables, captured by at least two indicators. The estimation results at the indicator level and at the level of the constructs are presented below.

Strategic variables

Global strategy is measured by two indicators: local sales and intrasystem sales. The operationalization of a construct by two indicators would lead to a negative number of degrees of freedom.[2] This problem can be solved by decreasing the number of parameters to be estimated, for instance, by assigning a fixed value to one or more parameters (e.g., $\lambda_1=1$), or by assuming that some parameters are equal (e.g., $\lambda_1=\lambda_2$) (see Bollen, 1989). Another solution is to estimate two constructs simultaneously. In this study, the latter route is followed. The rule used for combining constructs is the expectation that the constructs hardly influence one another. For all models with two constructs, additional tests were done with different combinations of constructs. These tests led to similar outcomes. Hence, the results of the confirmatory factor analyses are not influenced by the selection of the constructs that are estimated simultaneously.

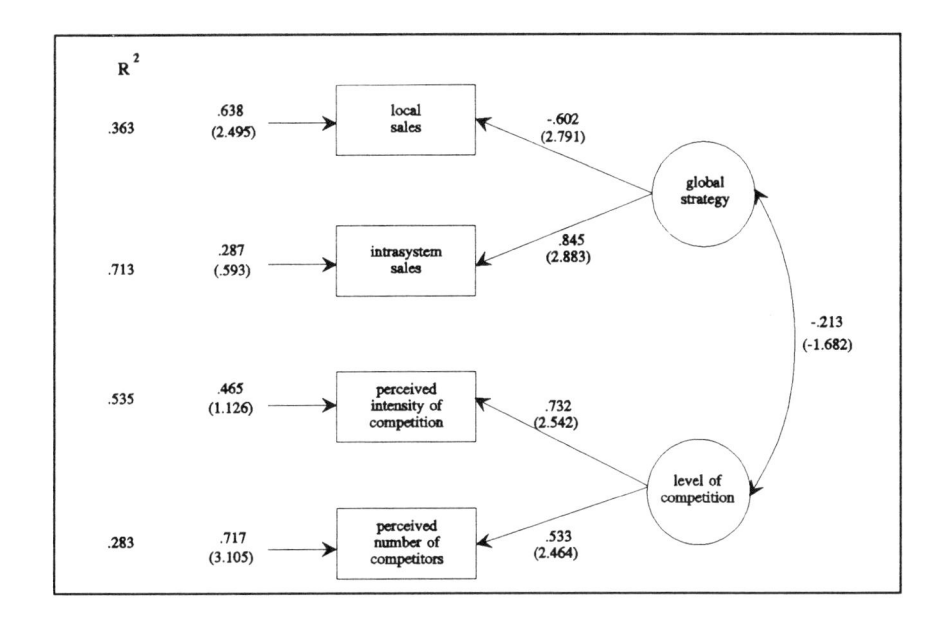

```
R²
         .638                 local         -.602
.363    (2.495)     ───▶     sales   ◀──   (2.791)
                                                      ┌─────────┐
                                                      │ global  │
                                                      │strategy │
                                                      └─────────┘
         .287              intrasystem    .845       ╱
.713    (.593)    ───▶       sales     ◀── (2.883)
                                                                    ╲
                                                                    -.213
                                                                   (-1.682)
         .465              perceived
.535    (1.126)   ───▶    intensity of  ◀── .732
                          competition       (2.542)
                                                      ┌─────────┐
                                                      │ level of│
                                                      │competit.│
                                                      └─────────┘
         .717              perceived     .533        ╱
.283    (3.105)   ───▶     number of   ◀── (2.464)
                          competitors
```

Figure 5.1 CFA maximum likelihood estimates of *global strategy* and *level of competition*

The construct *global strategy* was estimated together with latent variable *level of competition* (see Figure 5.1), with the covariances of the disturbance terms between these two constructs being fixed at zero. Figure 5.1 should be interpreted in the same way as Figure 4.1. The values in parentheses are t-values, and the reliability of each indicator is added under the heading 'R^2'. The results of the analysis indicate that the (convergent) validity of the indicators ($=\lambda_i$'s) is rather well: 0.602 and 0.845 for global strategy, and 0.732 and 0.533 for the level of competition. The t-values of all λ_i's exceed the value 2, which implies that these estimations are significant (see section 4.4). The reliability of the indicators ranges from 0.362 to 0.713 for global strategy and from 0.283 to 0.535 for the level of competition.

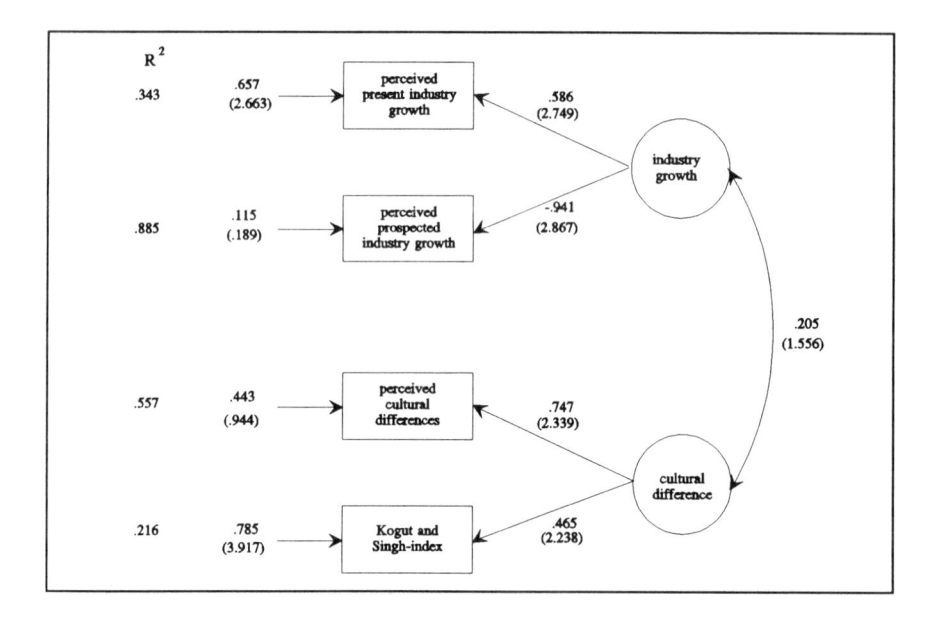

```
        R²                          perceived
       .343    .657         ────►  present industry  ◄────   .586
               (2.663)              growth                  (2.749)
                                                                        ┌─────────┐
                                                                        │ industry│
                                                                        │ growth  │
                                                                        └─────────┘
                                    perceived            -.941
       .885    .115         ────►  prospected   ◄────   (2.867)
               (.189)               industry growth

                                                                                    .205
                                                                                   (1.556)

                                    perceived
       .557    .443         ────►  cultural     ◄────    .747
               (.944)               differences         (2.339)
                                                                        ┌─────────┐
                                                                        │ cultural│
                                                                        │difference│
                                                                        └─────────┘
       .216    .785         ────►  Kogut and    ◄────    .465
               (3.917)              Singh-index         (2.238)
```

Figure 5.2 CFA maximum likelihood estimates of *industry growth* **and** *cultural difference*

The latent variable *industry growth* is measured by two indicators. Analogous to the construct *global strategy*, this construct was estimated simultaneously with another construct, viz. *cultural difference* (see Figure 5.2). Again, no covariance is assumed between the error terms of the constructs. Below, the results of *industry growth* are discussed; the results of *cultural difference* are postponed to the subsection where the locational variables are considered.

The indicators of the construct *industry growth* differ somewhat from one another with regard to validity and reliability. One indicator (chance of continuation of industry growth) is very reliable (0.885) and has a validity ($=\lambda$) of -0.941 with a t-value larger than 2. The other indicator (perceived present industry growth) has a lower reliability (0.343) and validity (0.586). Again, λ is significant.

Ownership-specific variables

Two ownership-specific variables are latent variables, viz. *international experience* and *host country experience*. The construct *international experience* is operationalized through three indicators (see Figure 5.3). This model has zero degrees of freedom. All three individual indicators have a highly significant λ, with a value that ranges from 0.733 to 0.910. The reliability of each indicator is fairly high: 0.537, 0.650, and 0.829.

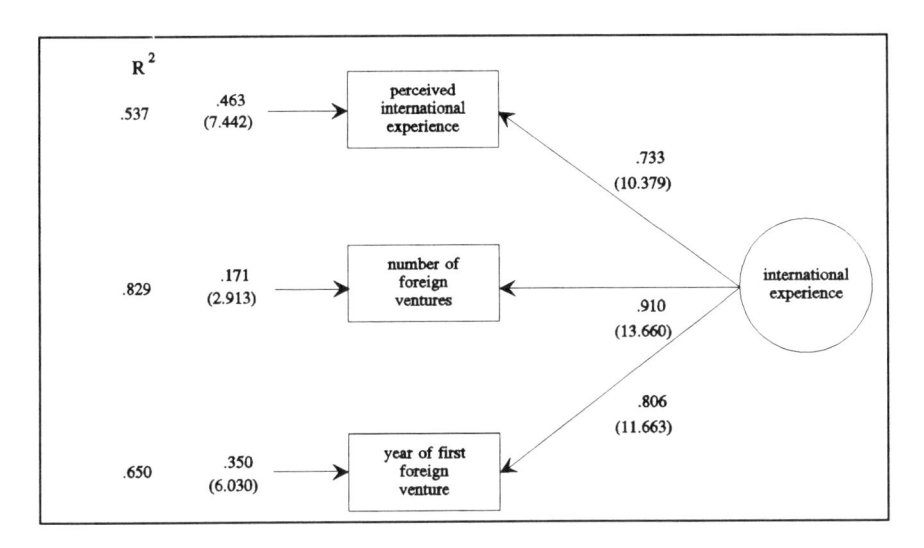

Figure 5.3 CFA maximum likelihood estimates of *international experience*

The second ownership-specific latent variable, *host country experience*, is measured by two indicators: the perceived familiarity with host country characteristics and the experience in the host country. To enable the estimation of this latent variable, the construct *reputation* was included in the confirmatory factor analysis (see Figure 5.4). The covariance between the disturbance terms of these constructs is assumed to be zero. The results of the latent variable *reputation* will be presented in the subsection where the transactional variables will be dealt with.

The two indicators of the construct *host country experience* have a rather high λ: 0.951 and 0.636, with t-values that are much higher than the threshold value of 2. The reliability is 0.903 and 0.404, respectively.

Transactional variables

The first transactional construct *reputation* was estimated simultaneously with the construct *host country experience*. The results of the model estimation are shown in Figure 5.4.

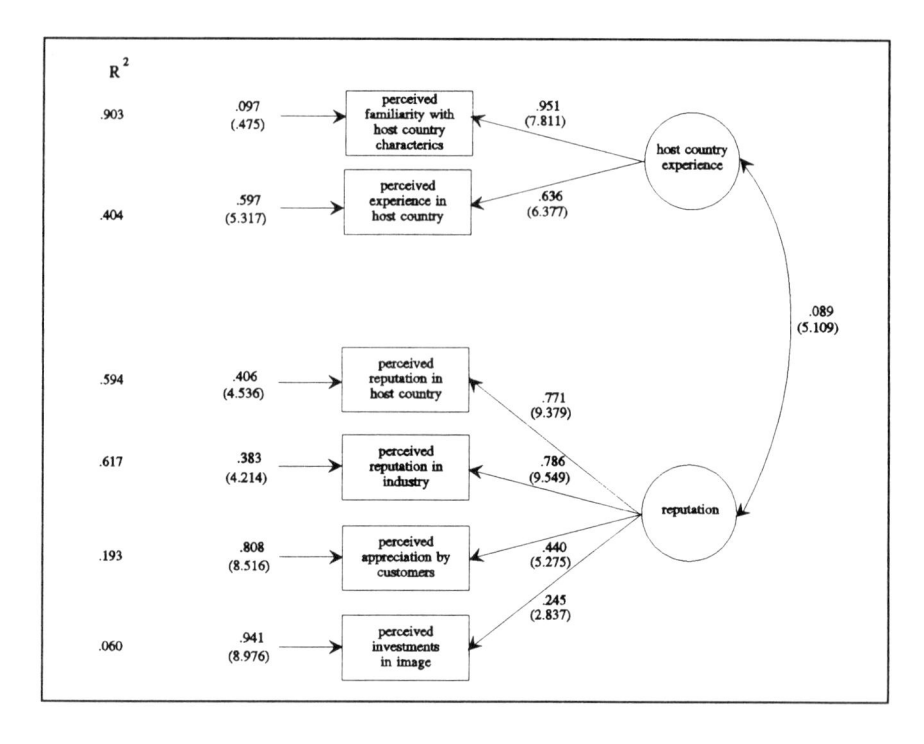

Figure 5.4 CFA maximum likelihood estimates of *host country experience* **and** *reputation*

Three indicators have a very significant λ: 0.771, 0.786, and 0.440. The fourth indicator 'perceived investments in image' has a rather low validity (λ=0.245), although the t-value of the λ is still above the threshold value. The reliability of this indicator is very low (0.060). Therefore, this indicator is left out of the further analyses. This confirmatory factor analytic model was estimated again with the three remaining indicators as an operationalization of the construct *reputation*. The R^2s of these indicators (0.594, 0.617, and 0.193) are satisfactory.

```
         R²                                               .706
                       .502      ┌──────────┐            (6.408)       ╭────────╮
       .498         (3.731)      │ perceived │ ◄──────────────────────│ specific │
                    ─────────►   │ specific  │                         │ assets   │
                                 │   skills  │                         ╰────────╯
                                 └──────────┘                             │
                                                          .786            │
                       .384      ┌──────────┐            (6.734)          │
       .617         (2.421)      │ perceived │ ◄────────────────────────  │
                    ─────────►   │ specific  │                            │
                                 │   skills  │                            │
                                 └──────────┘                             │
                          .247                                           .446
                        (3.571)                                         (4.650)
                                 ┌──────────────┐                         │
                       .575      │ perceived risk│                        │
       .425         (3.919)      │ of opportunism│ ◄──── .653             │
                    ─────────►   │   know how    │      (5.323)           │
                                 └──────────────┘                    ╭────────╮
                                                                     │ risk of │
                                                                     │opportunism│
                                                                     ╰────────╯
                                                          .854            │
                                 ┌──────────────┐        (5.829)          │
                       .271      │perceived risk│ ◄──────────────────────│
       .729         (1.182)      │of opportunism│
                    ─────────►   │    skills    │
                                 └──────────────┘
```

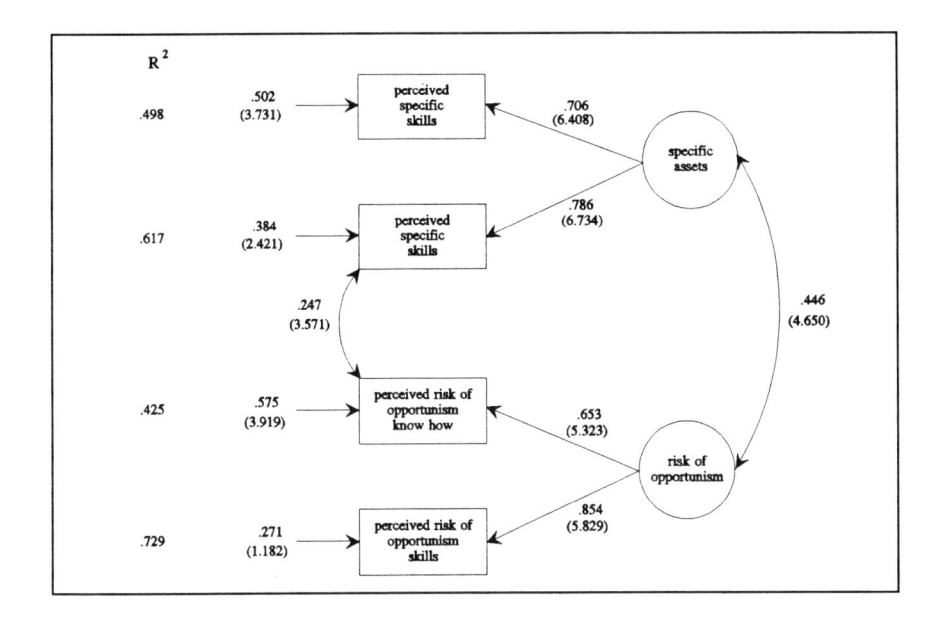

Figure 5.5 CFA maximum likelihood estimates of *specific assets* and *risk of opportunism*

The second transactional variable, *asset specificity*, is a dummy variable with the value 1 if the respondent's scores on the two latent variables *specific assets* and *risk of opportunism* are above the average scores on these variables. These two latent variables are operationalized by, in total, four indicators (see Figure 5.5). The covariance between the error terms of the indicators 'perceived specific know-how' and 'perceived risk of opportunism know-how' is not fixed to zero, but also estimated in the model. In this way, a possible relationship between these indicators can be captured. The reason for letting this covariance 'free' is that there may exist a relationship between asset specificity and the risk of opportunism. By including this covariance in the estimation model no degrees of freedom are left. Hence, the AGFI cannot be calculated, while the RMR and the largest fitted residual are equal to zero. All indicators have a highly significant λ, which ranges from 0.653 to 0.854. The indicators have a rather high reliability: 0.425, 0.498, 0.617, and 0.729.

Locational variables

Four locational variables are latent variables: cultural difference, host country risk, host government policy, and level of welfare. The construct *cultural difference* was measured by two indicators. This construct was estimated together with the construct *industry growth* in the confirmatory factor analysis (see Figure 5.2). The first indicator, 'perceived cultural differences', has a significant λ (0.747) and a rather high reliability ($R^2=0.557$). The second indicator, the 'Kogut and Singh index', or cultural distance according to Hofstede (1980, 1991), has a somewhat lower validity (λ=0.465) and reliability (0.216). Yet, the t-value of λ is larger than 2. The observation that the second indicator has a lower validity and reliability than the first indicator, 'perceived cultural differences', is important, because most empirical studies have used the Kogut and Singh index as the only indicator of cultural differences between a home and a host country (see, e.g., Agarwal, 1994; Agarwal and Ramaswami, 1992b; Benito and Gripsrud, 1992; Cho and Padmanabhan, 1995; Kogut and Singh, 1988a; Shane, 1994). Apparently, decision makers' perceptions of cultural differences deviate in a non-trivial way from the cultural distance based on the four dimensions of national culture as proposed by Hofstede (1980, 1991)![3]

The second locational construct, *host country risk*, is measured by four indicators (see Figure 5.6). The λ of each indicator is highly significant. The R^2s of all indicators are satisfactory, except the reliability of 'perceived political stability', which has a very high value: 0.831.

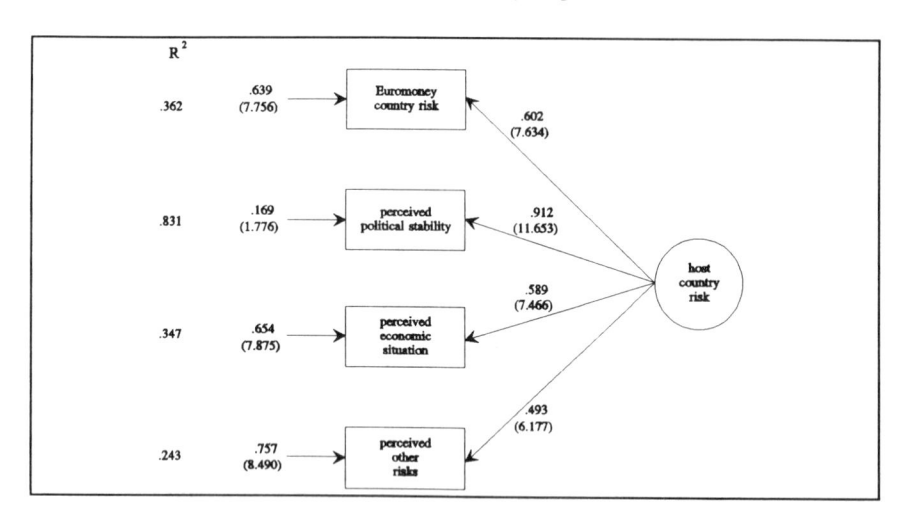

Figure 5.6 CFA maximum likelihood estimates of *host country risk*

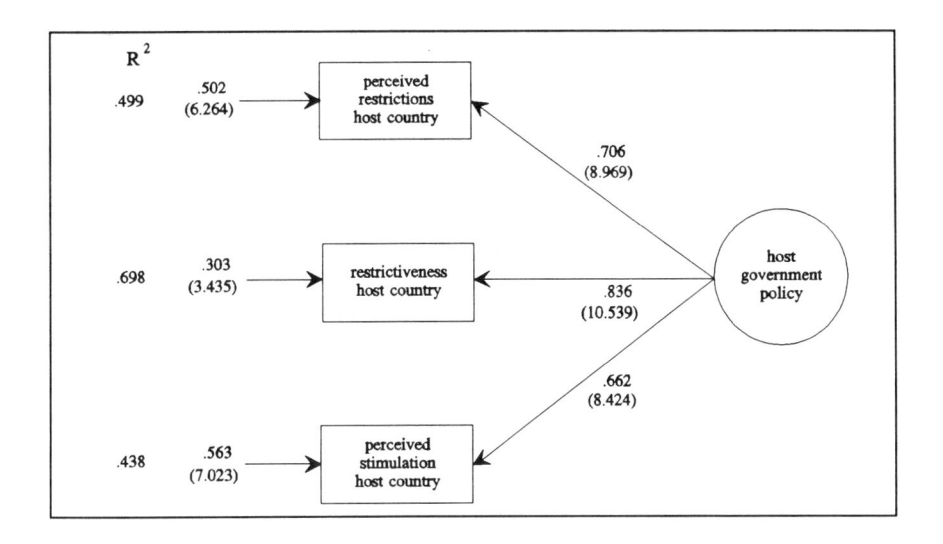

```
        R²
              .502          perceived
        .499  (6.264)  →   restrictions  ←
                          host country
                                            .706
                                           (8.969)
              .303         restrictiveness                  host
        .698  (3.435)  →   host country   ←                government
                                            .836            policy
                                          (10.539)
                                            .662
                                           (8.424)
              .563          perceived
        .438  (7.023)  →   stimulation   ←
                          host country
```

Figure 5.7 CFA maximum likelihood estimates of *host government policy*

The latent variable *host government policy* is proxied by three indicators, which resulted in a model without any degrees of freedom left. Figure 5.7 shows that each indicator has a highly significant λ. The reliability of each indicator is fairly high: 0.438, 0.499, and 0.698.

The last latent variable, *level of welfare*, is measured by five indicators (see Figure 5.8). Four out of five indicators have a highly significant λ, and a high R^2. The fifth indicator 'perceived level of knowledge of local firms' has a rather moderate validity (λ=0.297; t-value=3.793), but a very low reliability (R^2=0.088). As a result, this indicator will be excluded from the estimation of the construct *level of welfare*. This construct was re-estimated with the remaining four indicators, and the results were taken as the input for the second step: the testing of the relationships (see sections 5.3 to 5.5).

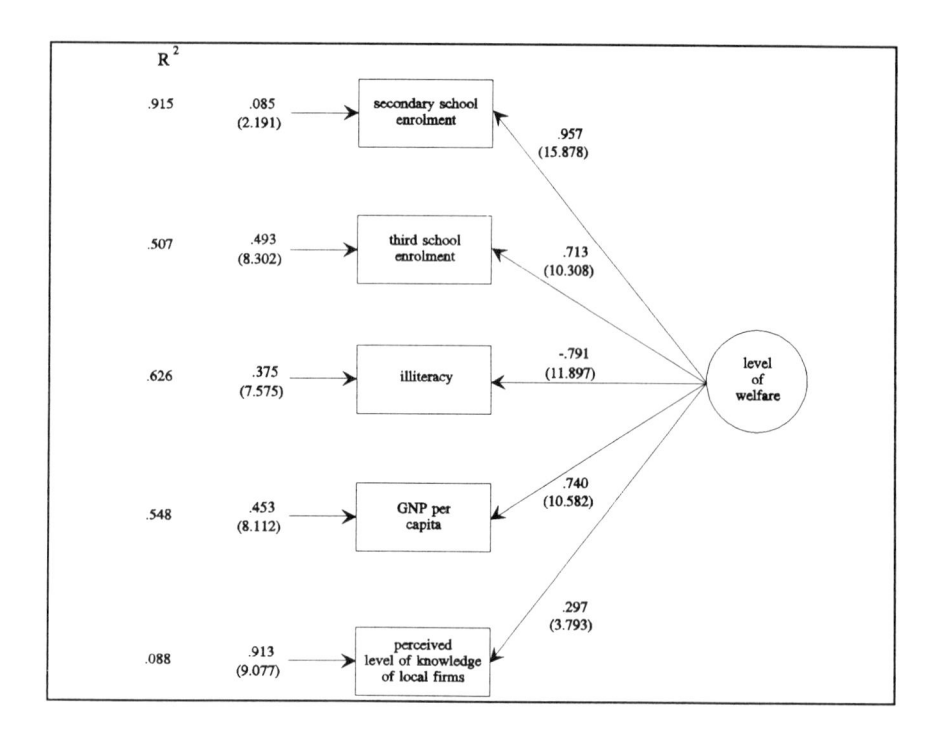

```
         R²
                                    ┌─────────────────┐
      .915        .085              │ secondary school│
                 (2.191)  ──────────▶│    enrolment    │◀─────┐  .957
                                    └─────────────────┘       │ (15.878)
                                                              │
                                    ┌─────────────────┐       │
      .507        .493              │   third school  │       │  .713
                 (8.302)  ──────────▶│    enrolment    │◀─────┤ (10.308)
                                    └─────────────────┘       │
                                                              │
                                    ┌─────────────────┐       │   ╭──────╮
      .626        .375              │                 │       │   │ level │
                 (7.575)  ──────────▶│    illiteracy   │◀─────┤   │  of   │
                                    └─────────────────┘   -.791 │welfare│
                                                         (11.897)╰──────╯
                                    ┌─────────────────┐       │
      .548        .453              │    GNP per      │       │  .740
                 (8.112)  ──────────▶│    capita       │◀─────┤ (10.582)
                                    └─────────────────┘       │
                                                              │
                                    ┌─────────────────┐       │  .297
                                    │   perceived     │       │ (3.793)
      .088        .913              │ level of knowledge│◀────┘
                 (9.077)  ──────────▶│  of local firms │
                                    └─────────────────┘
```

Figure 5.8 CFA maximum likelihood estimates of *level of welfare*

Construct and model evaluation

Table 5.1 summarizes the reliability and validity of all latent variables, and the four criteria for the evaluation of the model as a whole (see section 4.4). From this table it can be concluded that all constructs have a fairly high reliability and a somewhat lower - but still very satisfactory - validity. The validity is satisfactory but not very high, because of the relatively small number of indicators per construct. An increase in the number of relevant indicators generally leads to a higher validity of the constructs.

Furthermore, Table 5.1 clearly shows that all models have a very good fit:

1   Nearly all covariance of the models is explained by the model parameters (all AGFI's approach the maximum value 1).
2   The average of the variance of the residuals that cannot be explained by the models is negligible (all RMRs approach 0).
3   All indicators together appear to be very good measuring instru-

ments for the latent variables (all coefficients of determination are close to 1).
4 The values of the fitted residuals that are not explained by the models are far below the critical value of 0.1.

This section presented the results of the confirmatory factor analyses. Two indicators, each of which was expected to affect an underlying variable, turned out to be an unreliable measure of these constructs. Therefore, these indicators were omitted from the confirmatory factor analyses. The re-estimated models (i.e., without these two indicators) turned out to produce valid and reliable indicators. The results of these re-estimated models were used as input for the subsequent analyses.

Table 5.1
Overview of the reliability and validity of the constructs, and of the evaluation criteria of the CFA models

Latent variables	Reliability	Validity	AGFI	RMR	Coeff. of determ.	Largest fitted res.
Global strategy	0.694	0.538	0.934	0.022	0.901	0.028
Level of competition	0.575	0.410	0.934	0.022	0.901	0.028
Industry growth	0.751	0.614	0.975	0.015	0.956	0.016
International experience	0.860	0.672	---[1]	0.000	0.887	0.000
Host country experience	0.756	0.608	0.890	0.038	0.967	0.055
Reputation	0.682	0.458	0.890	0.038	0.967	0.055
Specific assets	0.715	0.557	---	0.000	0.939	0.000
Risk of opportunism	0.729	0.577	---	0.000	0.939	0.000
Cultural difference	0.545	0.387	0.975	0.015	0.956	0.016
Host country risk	0.752	0.446	0.974	0.021	0.864	0.028
Host government policy	0.780	0.545	---	0.000	0.803	0.000
Level of welfare	0.734	0.698	0.986	0.004	0.915	0.009

[1] If no degrees of freedom are left, LISREL cannot calculate the AGFI, while the RMR and the largest fitted residual are zero as in perfect models (Jöreskog and Sörbom, 1989). The coefficient of determination, however, can still be calculated for models without any degrees of freedom left.

5.3 Binomial logit analysis

This section presents the results of the binomial logit analysis. In the next sections, the results of two additional logit analyses (multinomial logit and ordered logit) will be presented. Together, these three analyses form the second step of the two-step approach: the testing of the hypotheses. First, however, the correlation matrix of all variables that are included in the logit analyses is given in Table 5.2.

Table 5.2
Means, standard deviations, and the correlation matrix of the dependent variable and the independent variables

		Mean	SD	1	2	3	4	5	6	7	8	9
1	Entry mode	.4464	.4986	1.0000								
2	Glob. strat.	.2006	.9055	-.1586	1.0000							
3	Lev. comp.	4.0732	1.3248	-.1389	-.1749	1.0000						
4	Ind. growth	-1.1135	1.0797	.1448	-.0438	-.1826	1.0000					
5	Intern. exp.	1.0366	.4009	-.1612	.0980	.0853	.0218	1.0000				
6	Host exp.	.7809	.6632	.1855	.0431	-.1240	.0273	-.0029	1.0000			
7	JV exp.	.3214	.4684	.7664**	-.0323	-.1400	.0965	-.2791**	.1214	1.0000		
8	WOS exp.	.4405	.4979	-.7968**	.0846	.1317	-.1426	-.0291	-.2350*	-.6107**	1.0000	
9	Prod. exp.	6.2381	1.4528	.0177	-.0059	-.0294	-.1264	.0194	.0304	-.0251	.0114	1.0000
10	Rel. size	2.1488	1.5958	-.1592	-.1302	.0422	.1645	.0042	-.1195	-.1765	.1431	.0466
11	Asset spec.	.3452	.4769	-.2234*	.1075	-.0105	.0175	.1455	-.0337	-.2378*	.0758	.0052
12	Reputation	2.6282	1.5998	-.1692	.4143**	.0415	-.0342	.2201*	.0964	-.1349	.0789	-.1029
13	Cult. diff.	2.2419	.9761	.1666	-.0586	-.1186	.0985	-.2837**	.2453*	.1734	-.0825	.0587
14	Host risk	5.0071	3.4189	.1429	-.0530	-.1061	-.0743	-.3871**	.2573**	.2099**	-.0646	.0548
15	Host pol.	.8930	1.7612	.1162	.3670**	-.1043	-.0400	-.1363	.0951	.0941	-.0889	.0076
16	Lev. of welf.	2.1479	1.5281	-.0754	.0513	.1882	-.0716	.3442**	-.2467*	-.1394	.0348	-.0653
17	Firm size	5.4488	2.9758	.0529	.0328	-.0309	-.0529	-.1170	-.0465	.0277	-.0459	-.0181
18	Advert. ind.	.2500	.4343	-.0760	.1764	.0629	.0297	.1395	.0030	-.1913	.0138	.0190
19	Knowl. ind.	.2738	.4472	.0662	-.0754	-.0138	.1585	-.1099	-.0851	.0633	-.0339	.0189
20	Res. ind.	.1905	.3939	-.1002	.0506	-.1094	-.0721	-.1009	-.1120	-.0417	.1803	.0249
21	Type of act.	4.1488	1.8463	.0770	.0533	-.0321	.1520	.0308	-.0437	.0482	-.0326	.0738

		10	11	12	13	14	15	16	17	18	19	20	21
10	Rel. size	1.0000											
11	Asset spec.	-.1502	1.0000										
12	Reputation	-.1429	.1881	1.0000									
13	Cult. diff.	-.1423	-.1013	-.1591	1.0000								
14	Host risk	-.2613**	-.0814	-.1824	.4951**	1.0000							
15	Host pol.	-.1390	-.1806	.1494	.1681	.2021*	1.0000						
16	Lev. of welf.	.1513	.0415	.1768	-.3572**	-.7205**	-.2000*	1.0000					
17	Firm size	-.1652	.0563	-.0332	.0857	-.0320	.1396	.0021	1.0000				
18	Advert. ind.	-.0022	.0304	.0841	-.0823	-.1163	.0579	.1865	.1138	1.0000			
19	Knowl. ind.	-.0071	-.0633	-.0488	.1397	.0084	.0205	-.0897	.0359	-.1696	1.0000		
20	Res. ind.	.0594	-.0048	-.1060	.0944	.1318	.0968	-.0982	.0474	.1400	-.1959	1.0000	
21	Type of act.	.1042	-.0583	.0270	.0665	-.0301	.1002	-.0337	.0971	.0877	.0736	.1172	1.0000

* $p < 0.01$; ** $p < 0.001$ (two-tailed).

In this correlation matrix, correlations are significant at the 0.01 (0.001) level if they have a value of at least 0.20 (0.25). A careful investigation of the correlation matrix learns that only four correlations are larger than |0.50|, while correlations above |0.60| are considered to be rather high (see, e.g., Churchill, 1991). Two of these correlations are between the dependent variable and an independent variable (*JV experience* and *WOS experience*). The high value of these correlations with the dependent variable (0.7664 and -0.7968) may cause multicollinearity. To find out whether multicollinearity problems would occur, three logit models were estimated including *JV experience*, *WOS experience*, and both, respectively. The results of all three binomial logit analyses revealed multicollinearity problems. Because of the multicollinearity effects, these variables (*JV experience* and *WOS experience*) will be left out of the logit analyses. Consequently, Hypothesis 6 on mode experience cannot be tested.

An additional effect of the elimination of these variables is that one of the other high correlations disappears. This particular correlation (-0.6107) was between *JV experience* and *WOS experience*. Hence, only one rather high correlation remains, viz. between *level of welfare* and *host country risk* (-0.7205). Two separate logit models were conducted: one without *level of welfare* and one without *host country risk*. The results of these models are comparable to the results of the whole model. However, the effect of *host country risk* is no longer significant when the *level of welfare* is omitted from the model. This suggests that the level of welfare needs to be controlled when measuring the impact of country risk, and vice versa. All other correlations are fairly low, making further exclusions of variables unnecessary.

Table 5.3 contains the logit estimates of β and its standard error (presented in parentheses) for each explanatory variable and control variable. Furthermore, the level of significance is provided for each variable.[4] Below, the results are discussed for all explanatory variables. Positive values of a regression coefficient means that the particular variable increases the probability of a JV compared to a WOS. A negative coefficient means that a WOS is more likely than a JV.

The first hypothesis that firms with a global strategy prefer a WOS to a JV when entering a foreign market is not corroborated. As expected, the effect of global strategy on the likelihood of JVs is negative ($\beta = -0.2328$). However, it is insignificant. This result suggests that a high-control entry mode (a WOS) is not required if the firm follows a global strategy. This insignificant effect is not in line with Kim and Hwang (1992), who found that more control is (significantly) preferred over less control in case global synergies can be achieved. They, however, did not compare JVs and WOSs directly. Hence, there is no evidence of a significant effect of a global strategy on the choice between JVs and WOSs.

Contrary to the expectation, a higher level of competition in the industry entered has a negative (-0.3463) and significant ($p < 0.05$) effect on the propensity to set up a JV. This implies a preference for a WOS in the case of high-competition industries. WOSs create extra capacities in an industry, which will most likely incite incumbent firms to react fiercely. Perhaps Dutch MNEs possess (or perceive that they possess) strong competitive advantages that may overcome the problems that arise from entering a highly competitive industry on their own (compare Hennart and Park, 1994; Yip, 1982). In general, MNEs have such distinctive advantages (see Hennart and Park, 1994; Teece, 1981) which may lead them to decide to enter a highly competitive industry on their own. To test this proposition, an additional logit model was calculated that included the interaction between international experience and the level of competition. International experience was taken as a proxy for the distinctive competitive advantages of MNEs. The logit analysis revealed that the negative coefficient of the level of competition remained negative, but the effect is no longer significant. The interaction effect also turned out to have an insignificant, negative effect on the incidence of JVs. A first preliminary conclusion based on these findings is that international experience appears to be not the only distinctive competitive advantage of Dutch MNEs, since the interaction effect was insignificant. Unfortunately, no other advantages of MNEs are included in the survey, which makes it impossible to test which competitive advantages (including international experience) increase the tendency to enter a highly competitive industry with a WOS.

The present study's finding that WOSs are preferred over JVs when a highly competitive industry is entered, conflicts with Gomes-Casseres's (1990) finding. He found a significant effect of the intensity of competition in the industry entered on the likelihood of JVs. So far, his study is the only study that found a significant impact of competition intensity on foreign entry mode choice. All other studies led to insignificant results in this respect (Hennart, 1991; Kim and Hwang, 1992; Kogut and Singh, 1988b; Larimo, 1993).

Table 5.3
Binomial logit estimations of the eclectic model: JVs vs. WOSs[1]

Independent variables	Coefficients
Intercept	4.9995***
	(2.0488)
Global strategy	-0.2328
	(0.3556)
Level of competition	-0.3463**
	(0.1880)
Industry growth	0.4034**
	(0.2165)
International experience	-0.9975*
	(0.6789)
Host country experience	0.6044*
	(0.3872)
Product experience	0.0609
	(0.1373)
Relative size	-0.3539**
	(0.1729)
Asset specificity	-0.8194**
	(0.4776)
Reputation	-0.2704*
	(0.1787)
Cultural difference	-3.0452***
	(1.2257)
(Cultural difference)^2	0.6655***
	(0.2656)
Host country risk	0.1941**
	(0.1059)
Host government policy	-0.0637
	(0.1446)
Level of welfare	0.5781***
	(0.2324)
Firm size	0.0418
	(0.0738)
Advertising-intensive industry	0.4925
	(0.5641)
Know-how-intensive industry	-0.0279
	(0.4787)
Resource-intensive industry	-0.7762
	(0.6180)
Type of activity (1) (R&D)	-0.0760
	(1.7242)
Type of activity (2) (production)	0.2218
	(0.7839)
Type of activity (3) (marketing and sales)	-1.5788***
	(0.6633)
Type of activity (4) (R&D + production)	-2.7182**
	(1.6108)
Type of activity (5) (R&D + marketing and sales)	-7.9058
	(20.3777)
Type of activity (6) (production + marketing and sales)	0.0369
	(0.6759)
Model-χ^2	71.066
Significance	0.0000
Degrees of freedom	24

* $p<0.1$; ** $p<0.05$; *** $p<0.01$ (one-tailed). Values in parentheses are standard errors.
[1] A positive coefficient means an increased likelihood of JVs.

In line with Hypothesis 3, firms rather set up a JV than a WOS when entering a fast-growing industry ($\beta=0.4034$; $p<0.05$). This finding suggests that JVs are better vehicles for capturing the benefits of market growth than WOSs (compare Hennart, 1991). JVs usually require less time than WOSs before they are in complete operation, because JVs may use existing facilities of their partners. This reduction in time is a comparative and competitive advantage of JVs (Stalk, 1988). As a result, JVs enable firms to quickly gain a good competitive position in rapidly growing industries.

Hypothesis 4 is also corroborated: firms with much international experience indeed have a higher inclination to set up WOSs ($\beta=-0.9975$; $p<0.1$). Experienced firms have become familiar with operating in a great many different environments. In addition, from earlier foreign entries they know what the potential pitfalls are of being a new player in an unknown market. Apparently, these firms have learnt how to deal with new contexts and how to adapt to the local contingencies. With an increase in cumulative international experience, the necessity of joining forces with a local partner decreases and, eventually, disappears. This finding is comparable with findings of previous studies (Agarwal, 1994; Agarwal and Ramaswami, 1992a, 1992b; Benito, 1996; Gatignon and Anderson, 1988; Madhok, 1994).

Contrary to the expected effect (see Hypothesis 5), experience in the host country significantly increases the probability of JVs as compared to WOSs ($\beta=0.6044$; $p<0.1$). Moreover, it is also in contrast with the effect of international experience. Apparently, international experience and host country experience are two really distinct, firm-specific capabilities. Different things are learnt from international expansions in general than from the experience a firm builds up in one host country.[5] On the one hand, firms with many foreign ventures have experience in dealing with foreign contexts and foreign firms. They have learnt which trajectory to follow when a new market is entered. On the other hand, firms with much experience in one host country are expected to have learnt how to deal with a host country's unique characteristics. This study's results, however, suggest that in spite of the increased host country experience, firms prefer a JV over a WOS. Apparently, firms are not afraid of establishing JVs with local firms when they see new opportunities in the host country. It seems that firms learn how to cooperate with firms in the host country, which may increase their likelihood of engaging in new JVs with local firms. This finding is in contrast with the results of previous studies (Gomes-Casseres, 1989, 1990; Hennart, 1991; Padmanabhan and Cho, 1994). Firms having no or only some host country experience turn out to prefer a WOS as the mode of entry. This initial preference may be due to the fact that inexperienced firms are unwilling to share control in an unknown and uncertain environment (see Davidson and McFetridge, 1985; Stopford and Wells, 1972). Another explanation may be that firms overestimate their own capabilities in understanding the local idiosyncrasies, or underestimate the difficulties of coping with them.

Hypothesis 7, which states that much product experience decreases the likelihood of JVs, is not confirmed. The effect of product experience on JVs ($\beta = 0.0609$) is insignificant. It seems that product experience or the direction of expansion has no impact on the choice between a JV and a WOS. To test whether there are differences between industries with regard to product experience, additional logit models were estimated with the interaction between product experience and the type of industry: advertising, know-how, and resource intensive (compare Gomes-Casseres, 1989). The results of these analyses indicate that a JV is more likely than a WOS ($p < 0.05$) when the industry entered fits within the core business of the firm, and is advertising intensive. No significant effects were found for the other types of industry.

Other studies also failed to find a significant effect for product experience (see, e.g., Gomes-Casseres, 1989; Larimo, 1993; Padmanabhan and Cho, 1994). However, some studies indeed confirmed that a JV is favoured over a WOS when the firm expands in a direction outside its core activities (Hennart, 1991; Hennart and Reddy, 1992; Stopford and Wells, 1972).

Unexpectedly, the relative size of the investment (Hypothesis 8) has a negative effect (-0.3539) on the probability that a JV is chosen, which is significant at the 0.05 level. A possible explanation for the preference of a WOS in the case of relatively large investments is to prevent a situation of unilateral dependence. Large subsidiaries will have a substantial impact on the MNE's performance. Then, full control may be preferred to secure that the subsidiary receives the attention and commitment it needs, and to prevent suboptimization and a deviation from the firm's interests. As a consequence, MNEs will select a WOS for such important affiliates to avoid becoming dependent on the unpredictable, and perhaps opportunistic, behaviour of a partner firm (Pfeffer and Salancik, 1978; Williamson, 1979, 1985). A necessary condition for using a WOS in such situations is that the MNE has enough resources (e.g., financial and managerial) to establish the foreign affiliate on its own.

This finding is in contrast with the outcomes of Kogut and Singh's study (1988b), which confirms that firms have a higher tendency to set up JVs when the foreign investment is large compared to the firms' size. So far, this latter study is the only study that found a significant effect of relative size on foreign entry mode choice.

The hypothesis that the specificity of the assets decreases the probability of JVs is supported ($\beta = -0.8194$; $p < 0.05$). This indicates that WOSs are better mechanisms than JVs to prevent the appropriation of specific know-how. This finding is in line with some other studies (Anderson and Gatignon, 1988; Erramilli and Rao, 1993; Padmanabhan and Cho, 1994). However, several empirical studies yielded an insignificant effect for asset specificity (see, e.g., Agarwal, 1994; Agarwal and Ramaswami, 1992b; Davidson and McFetridge, 1985; Fagre and Wells, 1972; Hennart, 1991). Subsequent logit analysis was done based on a modified version of this explanatory version that did not capture the risk of opportunistic behaviour. This analysis revealed that the effect of this modified variable was no longer significant, which implies that the risk of opportunistic behaviour is an essential condition for the selection of a WOS in the case of asset specificity.

As expected in Hypothesis 10, the firm's reputation has a significant, negative effect ($\beta = -0.2704$; $p < 0.1$) on the incidence of JVs. Firms that have a good image and reputation attempt to protect themselves from opportunistic behaviour of partner firms. This free-riding behaviour may deteriorate their reputation and even make all years of reputation building worthless. To prevent these negative externalities of cooperation, firms which have invested substantially in their reputation prefer to have full control over their expansions (Anderson and Gatignon, 1986; Brickley and Dark, 1987; Caves, 1982; Gatignon and Anderson, 1988; Stopford and Wells, 1972).

The effect of the cultural distance between the home country and the host country on the foreign entry mode choice was not specified in Hypothesis 11. The lopgit analysis showed that cultural distance had a positive, but not significant, effect on the likelihood of JVs. However, different forces may be relevant which cannot be adequately captured with a linear effect. Hence, a model was tested that included the square of cultural distance (see Table 5.3). The results in this table show a highly significant ($p < 0.01$) curvilinear effect: both small cultural differences and great cultural differences increase the likelihood of JVs (see Figure 5.9). This study is the first study that demonstrates that the relationship between cultural distance and foreign entry mode choice is more complex than is usually assumed. Dutch MNEs not only want to share equity in strange cultural settings, but also in cultures that resemble their home country's culture. Especially this second finding constitutes an interesting contribution to the foreign entry mode literature. It suggests that JVs are used for a diversity of purposes. In cultures dissimilar to the home country's culture, JVs are used as a means to get acquainted with the foreign culture, while in more similar cultures JVs are formed with firms for other reasons (e.g., joint research or cost reductions) than acculturation. Thus, firms are willing to cooperate with firms that have a comparable national culture, and also with firms that have a really different or complementary cultural background.

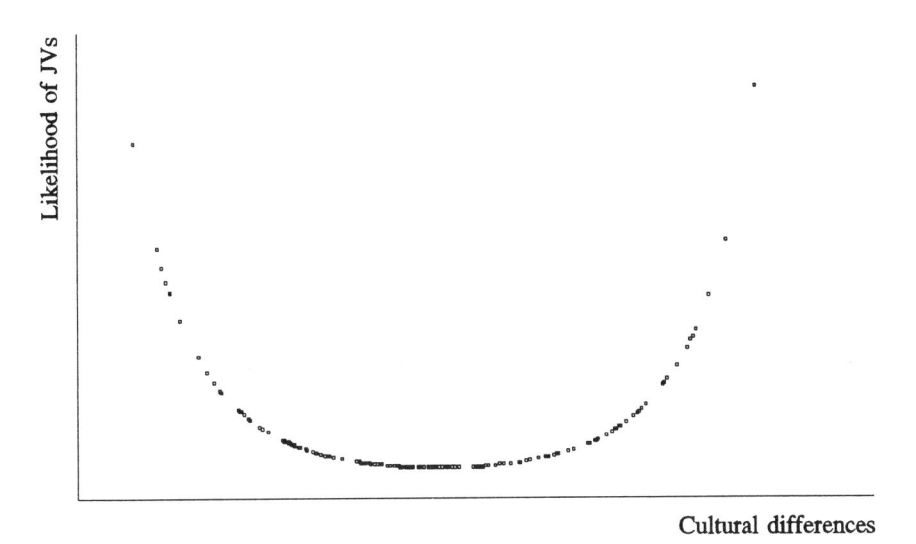

Figure 5.9 Effect of cultural differences on the likelihood of JVs

Most previous studies on US MNEs found that JVs are only preferred over WOSs when countries are entered which have a cultural background that differs substantially from the home country's culture (see, e.g., Agarwal, 1994; Davidson, 1982; Erramilli, 1991; Erramilli and Rao, 1993; Gatignon and Anderson, 1988; Kogut and Singh, 1988a). However, Japanese MNEs (Padmanabhan and Cho, 1994) prefer WOSs in the case of a greater cultural distance, and JVs in the case of a smaller cultural distance. Apparently, Dutch MNEs have something in common with American and Japanese MNEs, since they favour JVs if the cultural distance is either small or great.

According to Hypothesis 12, firms are expected to establish JVs in risky host countries. The binomial logit model confirms that such countries are entered with JVs ($\beta = 0.1941$; $p < 0.05$), presumably mainly to remain flexible in unstable and unpredictable conditions. This risk-averse behaviour of Dutch MNEs is consistent with that of American MNEs (Gatignon and Anderson, 1988; Kim and Hwang, 1992) and Norwegian MNEs (Benito, 1996). JVs are particularly appropriate to reduce potential losses when the firm's opportunities in a host country have vanished completely because of, for instance, a major shift in the political or economic situation. Compared with a WOS, the losses in a JV are divided between at least two firms.

A restrictive host government was believed to increase the likelihood of JVs (see Hypothesis 13). However, the analysis reveals that host government policy has no significant impact on the entry mode choice. This finding suggests that for Dutch firms in the late 1980s and early 1990s, the policy of host country governments is no longer a decisive factor for the formation of JVs. This is completely in line with the increasing relaxation of restrictive policies that can be observed since the mid-1980s (Contractor, 1990b).

Previous studies which found that restrictions significantly affect the likelihood of JVs have different time frames than the present study. This study focuses on foreign entries that had recently been established at the time of data collection (1993). Gatignon and Anderson (1988) and Gomes-Casseres (1989, 1990) used data on foreign entries before 1975, while Shane (1993) investigated entries that existed in 1977 and 1982. They all found that the restrictiveness of host governments had a significant influence on the likelihood of JVs. Padmanabhan and Cho (1994) used a database that contains data on Japanese entries between 1969 and 1991. They tested their model on two subsamples: entries before 1986 and from 1986 onwards. Their results showed that a restrictive government policy increases the chance of JVs significantly in both periods. However, the effect is much greater in the first period than in the second period (2.255 and 0.741, respectively).

The level of welfare in the host country was expected to have a positive effect on the likelihood of JVs (see Hypothesis 14). Table 5.3 shows that this hypothesis is confirmed: the level of welfare turns out to have a very significant ($p<0.01$), positive impact on the propensity to set up JVs ($\beta=0.5781$). It seems that, for Dutch firms, developed countries are more attractive to enter with JVs than developing countries. Local firms in developed countries can offer foreign MNEs more than local firms in developing countries can do. In this respect, two advantages are especially valuable: the commercial experience of local firms[6] (Gomes-Casseres, 1989) and the well-educated indigenous population. The positive effect of the level of welfare on the incidence of JVs is in line with the results of earlier studies (see Gomes-Casseres, 1989, 1990; Kobrin, 1987; Larimo, 1993; Shane, 1993).

The logit model, which converged after six iterations, appears to be a very good model, as it classifies 76.79 per cent of the observations correctly (see Table 5.4). This is significantly better than a random model would have achieved. A random model's classification rate is $\alpha^2 + (1-\alpha)^2$, with α being the number of JVs divided by the total number of observations (i.e., $73/168 = 0.4345$). In this study, a random model has an overall classification rate of 50.86 per cent. The relative classification improvement of the estimated model as opposed to a random model is: $(76.79 - 50.86) : 50.86 = 50.98$ per cent. This relative information gain is significantly higher than the minimal improvement of 25 per cent that is proposed by Hair et al. (1979). The sensitivity rate of the model, which indicates the ability of the model to correctly classify JVs, is quite high (70.67 per cent). The model classifies WOSs better than JVs (the specificity rate is 81.72 per cent). Models with a logistic distribution always tend to overclassify the category with the largest number of observations (Amemiya, 1981).[7]

Table 5.4
Classification table of the binomial logit analysis

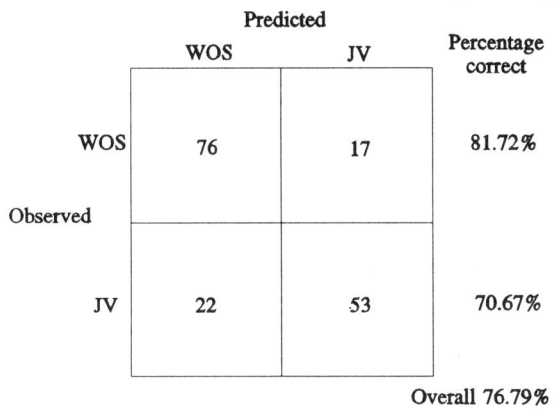

		Predicted		Percentage correct
		WOS	JV	
Observed	WOS	76	17	81.72%
	JV	22	53	70.67%

Overall 76.79%

The -2LL and the model-χ^2 also show that the model has a very high overall explanatory power (see Table 5.3). The null hypothesis that the model fits the perfect model cannot be rejected (-2LL is 159.899; p=0.1583). The model-χ^2 is 71.066 and highly significant (p=0.0000), which indicates a very good fit of the model. The ρ^2 is 0.31, which is also very acceptable.

The conclusion of the logit analysis on the eclectic model (see Table 5.3) is that the eclectic model can predict the choice of the foreign entry mode fairly well: the percentage of correct classifications is high and the model-χ^2 is highly significant.

Table 5.5
Binomial logit estimations of the separate theories: JVs vs. WOSs[1]

Independent variables	Strategic	Ownership-specific	Transactional	Locational
Intercept	2.1730**	1.8429*	0.8603	1.0057
	(0.9867)	(1.3118)	(0.6813)	(1.2123)
Global strategy	-0.5543**			
	(0.2963)			
Level of competition	-0.3334**			
	(0.1550)			
Industry growth	0.1694			
	(0.1730)			
International experience		-1.4444***		
		(0.5607)		
Host country experience		0.4564*		
		(0.3036)		
Product experience		0.0958		
		(0.1295)		
Relative size		-0.3353**		
		(0.1483)		
Asset specificity			-0.8086**	
			(0.4041)	
Reputation			-0.2314**	
			(0.1339)	
Cultural difference				-3.1933***
				(1.0287)
(Cultural difference)^2				0.7421***
				(0.2252)
Host country risk				0.2180***
				(0.0892)
Host government policy				-0.0302
				(0.1134)
Level of welfare				0.3722**
				(0.1908)
Firm size	0.0567	0.0069	0.0551	0.0524
	(0.0591)	(0.0634)	(0.0581)	(0.0645)
Advertising-intensive ind.	0.3702	0.3852	0.1655	0.3993
	(0.4547)	(0.4655)	(0.4398)	(0.4709)
Know-how-intensive ind.	0.1122	0.0119	0.0426	0.1427
	(0.4081)	(0.4208)	(0.4079)	(0.4248)
Resource-intensive ind.	-0.8521*	-0.7877*	-0.8909**	-0.7328*
	(0.5428)	(0.5508)	(0.5398)	(0.5451)
Type of activity (1)	0.3856	0.5302	0.5632	-0.3489
	(1.7169)	(1.5530)	(1.5533)	(1.6070)
Type of activity (2)	0.4979	0.0124	0.2901	0.3550
	(0.6332)	(0.6657)	(0.6295)	(0.6476)
Type of activity (3)	-1.0950**	-1.6866***	-1.1649**	-1.4274***
	(0.5516)	(0.5877)	(0.5446)	(0.5488)
Type of activity (4)	0.1750	-1.7333*	-0.2837	-1.8200*
	(1.1600)	(1.2786)	(1.1263)	(1.3763)
Type of activity (5)	-7.0896	-8.9809	-7.7770	-7.4147
	(20.8764)	(18.4041)	(20.8221)	(21.0636)
Type of activity (6)	0.0057	-0.2333	-0.0401	-0.1043
	(0.5769)	(0.5955)	(0.5725)	(0.5966)
Model-χ^2	31.848	39.624	31.750	44.315
Significance	0.0025	0.0003	0.0015	0.0001
Degrees of freedom	13	14	12	15

* $p<0.1$; ** $p<0.05$; *** $p<0.01$ (one-tailed). Values in parentheses are standard errors.
[1] A positive coefficient means an increased likelihood of JVs.

In the remainder of this section, the eclectic model developed in this study will be compared with the four separate theories that together constitute the cornerstones of the eclectic model. First, the parameter estimates of the individual theories will be presented (Table 5.5), afterwards all possible combinations of the four theoretical approaches are evaluated on their predictive quality (see Table 5.6).

Table 5.5 contains the estimates of the coefficients for each of the four theories with the same control variables as in the full model. The four partial models have a significant model-χ^2, which indicates that not all β's are zero.

In itself, the separate models are rather good models, but not so well as the complete eclectic model. The results of these partial models are to a large extent analogous to the results of the full model. Only one variable (industry growth), which was significant in the full model, is no longer significant, whereas one variable (global strategy), which was insignificant in the complete model, turned out to have a significant effect in the partial model including the strategic variables. All variables remained positive or negative, as they were before. This substantial overlap demonstrates that the variables which are significant in partial models are hardly influenced by other variables in the whole model. Hence, multicollinearity appears to be absent in the eclectic model. This also suggests that partial models result in relatively unbiased estimates of the effects.

In Table 5.6, the model-χ^2's of the separate theories and all possible combinations of these theories are compared with the model-χ^2 of the full eclectic model. Also, the percentages of correct classification of the entry modes of all models are presented. This table shows that the full eclectic model is superior to each of the individual theories in predicting the selected mode of foreign entry. The improvement in the model-χ^2 is highly significant. Thus, it is proved that the eclectic model, which was built in Chapter 3, is not only conceptually, but also statistically superior to one-sided approaches. Furthermore, it is evident from Table 5.6 that the combination of all four theoretical approaches leads to significantly better predictions than any combination of two or three of these approaches. Hence, the eclectic model proposed in the present study turns out to be a very good model.

So far, the results of the binomial logit analyses have been discussed. As argued before, in addition to a dichotomous dependent variable, it is also possible to distinguish four categories within the dependent variable: minority JV, 50/50 JV, majority JV, and WOS. In the next section, the results of the logit analyses with the categorized dependent variable will be discussed.

Table 5.6
Model-χ^2's, degrees of freedom, classification rates for all possible models, and a comparison with this study's eclectic model

Models (s=1 to 14)	Model-χ^2_s	Degrees of freedom	% of Correct classification	Improvement ($\chi^2_{Full} - \chi^2_s$)	Degrees of freedom[1]
Full model	71.066***	24	76.79	---	---
1. Strategic	31.848***	13	64.29	39.218***	11
2. Ownership-specific	39.624***	14	69.64	31.442***	10
3. Transactional	31.750***	12	66.67	39.316***	12
4. Locational	44.315***	15	73.81	26.751***	9
5. 1 + 2	47.687***	17	72.62	23.379***	7
6. 1 + 3	41.172***	15	72.02	29.894***	9
7. 1 + 4	55.859***	18	76.19	15.207**	6
8. 2 + 3	50.350***	16	74.40	20.716***	8
9. 2 + 4	53.788***	19	72.62	17.278***	5
10. 3 + 4	50.053***	17	71.43	20.013***	7
11. 1 + 2 + 3	57.235***	19	76.79	13.831**	5
12. 1 + 2 + 4	64.428***	22	77.38	6.638**	2
13. 1 + 3 + 4	61.431***	20	77.38	9.635**	4
14. 2 + 3 + 4	62.049***	21	73.81	9.017**	3

* $p < 0.1$; ** $p < 0.05$; *** $p < 0.01$
[1] This column contains the difference between the degrees of freedom of the full model and of each separate model.

5.4 Multinomial logit analysis

Following Gatignon and Anderson (1988), a more refined logit model was developed with a more specific breakdown in different types of JVs. It was expected that the effects of the explanatory variables are not equal for the distinct types of JV. A multinomial logit model enables a detailed investigation of whether and how effects differ for each type of JV. In this section, it is assumed that the dependent variable is an unordered categorical variable.

Multinomial logit analysis was carried out for two different methods of categorizing the dependent variable. First, the division of equity was taken as a criterion for dividing the JVs into the categories minority, 50/50, and majority. Second, the level of actual control was used for the allotment. See Table 5.7 for the number of observations that resulted in the two cases. Both models will be discussed below.

Table 5.7
The number of minority, 50/50, and majority JVs based on the division of equity and the division of control

	Based on control majority	50/50	minority	
Based on equity majority	17	1	4	22
50/50	8	23	4	35
minority	2	4	12	18
	27	28	20	

The distribution of the ventures in Table 5.7 demonstrates clearly that an equal division of the equity of a JV does not necessarily imply that both partners exert the same influence within the JV (compare Geringer and Hebert, 1989; Killing, 1983).

Table 5.8
Multinomial logit model with JVs grouped according to the level of equity[1]

Entry mode	Intercept	Global strategy	Level of welfare	Host policy	Level of compet.	Firm size	Industry growth	Advert. industry	Internat. exper.	Knowl. industry	Host exper.	Resource industry	Product exper.	Activity 1	Relative size	Activity 2	Asset spec.	Activity 3	Reputa-tion	Activity 4	Cult. diff.	Activity 5	(Cult. diff.)²	Activity 6	Host risk
Minority JV	7.2172** (3.6784)	0.0023 (0.6633)	0.4144 (0.3370)	0.3328 (0.2847)	−0.4967* (0.2968)	0.2252 (0.2909)	0.1422 (0.3379)	−0.6266 (1.1093)	0.0798 (1.2369)	−1.2359* (0.8828)	0.3817 (0.6288)	−0.4267 (1.0636)	−0.2009 (0.2165)	3.1078 (2.6167)	−1.6662*** (0.5981)	0.3971 (1.3053)	−0.5702 (0.8330)	−1.6604 (1.2264)	−0.1442 (0.2786)	−2.4191 (2.4821)	−4.5536*** (1.6441)	−9.8263# (.)	0.8934*** (0.3390)	0.8831 (1.2683)	0.0696 (0.1610)
50/50 JV	4.1162 (3.2897)	−0.4788 (0.4755)	0.8679*** (0.3054)	−0.2826* (0.1493)	−0.6688*** (0.2651)	0.0093 (0.2447)	0.5064** (0.2735)	0.6614 (0.7367)	−0.9516 (0.8860)	0.1896 (0.5829)	0.9014** (0.5211)	−1.1585* (0.8533)	0.1437 (0.1831)	−8.4862# (.)	−0.2200 (0.2165)	0.3213 (0.9007)	−0.6885 (0.6017)	−1.8978** (0.8122)	−0.3938** (0.2358)	−10.9077# (.)	−2.9147* (1.5703)	−7.9618# (.)	0.6750** (0.3266)	0.0087 (0.8053)	0.2687** (0.1350)
Majority JV	4.5523 (3.7587)	0.9463* (0.6022)	0.6896** (0.3312)	−0.0133 (0.2541)	0.1797 (0.2942)	−0.6435*** (0.2586)	0.4667 (0.3071)	1.7526** (0.8313)	−2.5144*** (1.0321)	0.1724 (0.7279)	0.8784 (0.6921)	−0.3161 (0.9263)	0.1088 (0.2273)	−5.6948# (.)	−0.1016 (0.2730)	1.1869 (1.2940)	−1.0344 (0.8474)	−1.0354 (1.0944)	−0.4813* (0.2985)	−2.7241 (2.1772)	−4.7901** (1.6390)	−8.2591# (.)	1.0700*** (0.3427)	1.2827 (1.1316)	0.3178** (0.1529)
WOS	0	0	0	0	0	0	0	0	0	0	0	0	0	0	0	0	0	0	0	0	0	0	0	0	0

* $p<0.1$; ** $p<0.05$; *** $p<0.01$ (one-tailed); # infinite parameters, due to a lack of JVs involved in these activities. Values in parentheses are standard errors.
[1] A positive coefficient means an increased likelihood of the specific type of JV relative to a WOS.

Table 5.8 contains the results of the multinomial logit analysis with the level of equity as the determinant of the categorization. Analogous to the binomial logit model, the WOS option is taken as the reference category. This means that the effects of the independent variables on the three types of JV should be interpreted as the effect relative to WOSs.[8]

The results of the multinomial logit analysis show that a global strategy has a significant effect ($\beta=0.9463$; $p<0.1$) on the propensity to choose a majority-owned JV over a WOS. This suggests that with a majority stake, the control required for a global strategy can be better ensured than with full ownership. A high level of competition significantly increases the likelihood of WOSs as opposed to 50/50 JVs ($\beta=-0.6688$; $p<0.01$) and minority JVs ($\beta=-0.4967$; $p<0.05$). Apparently, Dutch MNEs prefer to fully control entries in highly competitive markets. As such, they want to prevent that their firm-specific advantages are going to be acquired by other firms (see section 5.3). Table 5.8 reveals that especially 50/50 JVs ($\beta=0.5064$; $p<0.05$) and majority JVs ($\beta=0.4667$; $p<0.1$) are used to enter rapidly growing industries. This suggests that the bargaining position of the partner which is already present in the industry is so weak that no majority share can be obtained.

Firms with much international experience have a significant ($p<0.01$) preference for WOSs over majority JVs. Both other JV types have no significant effects. These results indicate that internationally experienced firms rather have full control over their new entries than share the control with another firm. Even a small share in the hands of a partner may lead to coordination problems, and may cause delays in the decision-making processes. In contrast, 50/50 JVs ($\beta=0.9014$; $p<0.05$) are favoured over WOSs when firms are highly experienced in the host country. As suggested in section 5.3, full comprehension of the specific local circumstances cannot be achieved on one's own. The input of a local partner remains a prerequisite, even for experienced MNEs. No significant effects are found for the variable product experience. With regard to the relative size of the investments, it turns out that WOSs are significantly appreciated over minority JVs ($\beta=-1.6662$; $p<0.01$) when relatively large investments are needed. This implies that a minority share will be avoided for such important subsidiaries.

The specificity of the assets transferred to the foreign affiliate has no significant effect on the different types of JV. This is strange, since the binomial logit model showed that asset specificity has a significant effect on the likelihood of WOSs. A firm's reputation is based on many years of image building, which usually involves the investment of a great deal of money. Firms with a good reputation prefer WOSs over all types of JVs when entering a foreign country. Especially 50/50 JVs and majority

JVs (significant at the 0.05 level and the 0.1 level, respectively) are less likely than WOSs, because in these governance structures partner firms can heavily abuse the MNE's reputation while only a relatively low investment is required.

The curvilinear effect of cultural differences on the likelihood of JVs holds for all three types of JVs. Thus, when compared to WOSs all three types of JVs are more likely as modes of entry in both culturally similar and culturally dissimilar countries. However, the effect of minority and majority JVs differs from the effect of 50/50 JVs (compare the β's of the variables *cultural differences* and *(cultural differences)²* for all three types of JVs). When the host country is very risky, 50/50 JVs and majority JVs are favoured over WOSs ($\beta=0.2687$ and $\beta=0.3178$, respectively; $p<0.05$). The insignificant effect of country risk on minority JVs is somewhat unexpected. Particularly in risky environments, firms are assumed to minimize their commitment in a way that the maximum loss is limited. Minority JVs are appropriate governance structures to achieve this aim. Perhaps risky host countries do not have a strong collection of indigenous firms which possess enough resources and capabilities to become a majority shareholder of a JV with a foreign firm. The restrictive policies of a host government lead to a significant ($\beta = -0.2826$; $p<0.05$) preference of WOSs over 50/50 JVs. This suggests that MNEs rather set up a WOS than an imposed 50/50 JV. Finally, particularly 50/50 JVs ($\beta=0.8679$; $p<0.01$) and majority JVs ($\beta=0.6896$; $p<0.05$) are selected when developed countries are entered. This finding supports the argumentation put forward in section 5.3, that firms in developed countries can offer foreign firms more than firms in developing countries.

The model as a whole turns out to be a good model (-2LL is 263.66, with $p=1.0000$), with a model-χ^2 of 126.00 which is highly significant ($p<0.001$), and $\rho^2=0.43$. The results of the multinomial logit analysis based on the division of equity resemble those of the binomial logit analysis. All variables that were significant in the binomial logit analysis are also significant (with the same sign) for at least one type of JV in the multinomial logit model, with one exception: *asset specificity*. In the binomial logit model, this variable turned out to have a significant effect on the incidence of WOSs, but in the multinomial logit model no significant influence was found. Furthermore, the insignificant variables of the binomial model are again insignificant, except for the variable *host government policy*, which turns out to be significant in the multinomial model. The multinomial model provides detailed information on the types of JV that are significantly affected by the explanatory variables. Table 5.8 clearly demonstrates that JVs should not be considered as one group of organizational forms. On the contrary! There are substantial differences among the various types of JVs (compare Bell and Jagersma, 1996; Killing, 1983).

In addition to this multinomial logit analysis based on the division of equity, a comparable analysis was carried out based on the division of control. Table 5.9 contains the results of this multinomial logit analysis that are largely similar to the model based on equity division. Here, only the differences between the two models with regard to significant effects will be discussed.

The second multinomial model shows no significant effect for the global strategy of firms on the entry mode choice, whereas majority-owned JVs were significantly preferred to WOSs in the first model. This suggests that a majority stake in the equity of the JV gives the firm full control over the venture which is needed when the firm has a global strategy.

In the second multinomial model, WOSs are not only more likely than majority JVs, which is the same outcome as in the first model, but also more likely than 50/50 JVs when the firm has much international experience. Obviously, these internationally experienced firms do not want to share control over their foreign ventures. According to Table 5.8, 50/50 JVs are preferred to WOSs when they have experience with the country to be entered. However, when the level of control is used to classify JVs, it appears that most of the control is in the hands of the local partner. Presumably, the local partner needs a high level of control over the venture to be able to adapt to the local idiosyncrasies. Equal division of the equity may serve as a sign of good intentions. When the investment is relatively large, firms turn out to have a significant preference for WOSs over both minority- and majority-controlled JVs. The first model indicates that WOSs are only preferred to minority-owned JVs.

In the multinomial logit model based on the division of equity, the specificity of the assets transferred in the relationship has no significant effect on any of the JV types. However, a high asset specificity turns out to influence significantly the propensity to engage in WOSs relative to 50/50- and majority-controlled JVs. Even the ability to control the JV to a large extent is not enough to prevent opportunistic behaviour. The significant negative effect of the firm's reputation on 50/50 JVs is no longer significant in the second multinomial logit model. This implies that WOSs are only preferred to majority JVs by firms which have heavily invested in their brand-name capital. Apparently, a 50 per cent equity stake was not enough to keep the partner from behaving in an opportunistic way, whereas truly equally shared control is believed to do so.

The U-shaped relationship between cultural differences and 50/50 JVs is not significant any more when the level of control is used instead of the level of equity. The signs are still as expected. This finding suggests that sharing the equity equally is necessary when the culture is quite similar (as an expression of mutual trust) or rather dissimilar (as a sign of good intentions). The control, however, is not really shared equally between partners in the case of either a small or a great cultural distance. In such situations, it seems important to have one firm that largely controls the JV. The last differences involve the effects of the host government's policy on the preference for WOSs. WOSs are more likely than majority-controlled JVs ($p < 0.05$) when the local government puts restrictions on foreign ownership. The significant effect of the likelihood of WOSs as opposed to 50/50 JVs (see Table 5.8) is no longer significant in the second model. Apparently, sharing control equally with a local partner in a restrictive country is not a realistic option for Dutch MNEs, because of all potential problems related to the coordination and communication required. The results of the second multinomial logit model indicate that if firms are in a position to acquire most of the control of a JV that is established to meet local restrictive policies, they prefer to set up a WOS. In that case, they do not have any coordination problems with an imposed partner.

Again, the null hypothesis that the model is not significantly different from the perfect model cannot be rejected (-2LL is 277.53; p=1.0000). The model-χ^2 is 116.65 with $p < 0.0001$, and $\rho^2 = 0.40$.

The overall results of the multinomial logit models are comparable to the results of the binomial logit model. The multinomial logit analyses added insight into the differences among the three types of JVs. It has clearly been demonstrated that JVs should not be considered as one group, since there are many differences among minority JVs, 50/50 JVs, and majority JVs. Furthermore, the multinomial logit analyses revealed that differences exist between the classification of JVs on equity and control. For example, majority-owned JVs are not always identical to majority-controlled JVs. Both models are good models: the -2LL's are insignificant, the model-χ^2's are highly significant, whereas the measures of overall fit (ρ^2) are 0.43 and 0.40, respectively. In the next section, the results of the multinomial logit models will be contrasted with those of the ordered logit models to find out which of these models fits the data best.

Table 5.9
Multinomial logit model with JVs grouped according to the level of control[1]

Entry mode	Intercept	Global strategy	Level of compet.	Firm size	Industry growth	Internat. exper.	Host exper.	Product exper.	Relative size	Asset spec.	Reputa-tion	Cult. diff.	(Cult. diff.)[2]	Host risk
Minority JV	4.3851 (3.6568)	-0.1231 (0.6437)	-0.4281* (0.3048)	0.1810 (0.2813)	-0.1025 (0.3196)	-0.4743 (1.0595)	1.0392* (0.7328)	0.1669 (0.2469)	-1.1184*** (0.4577)	0.0145 (0.8380)	-0.3119 (0.2954)	-4.3293** (1.5994)	0.8508*** (0.3350)	0.1149 (0.1556)
50/50 JV	2.2231 (3.5659)	-0.5169 (0.4638)	-0.5019** (0.2566)	-0.0426 (0.2514)	0.4559* (0.3007)	-1.2888* (0.8884)	0.5783 (0.5022)	0.2025 (0.2108)	-0.2062 (0.2254)	-1.0797* (0.6987)	-0.1999 (0.2351)	-1.9285 (1.6157)	0.5132* (0.3325)	0.2246* (0.1423)
Majority JV	9.5882*** (3.3608)	0.5132 (0.5127)	-0.2218 (0.2513)	-0.5443** (0.2408)	0.7130*** (0.2858)	-1.6814** (0.9412)	0.5683 (0.5320)	-0.0712 (0.1735)	-0.3388* (0.2334)	-1.0268* (0.6880)	-0.4923** (0.2619)	-4.1495*** (1.4732)	0.9180*** (0.3144)	0.1871* (0.1411)
WOS	0	0	0	0	0	0	0	0	0	0	0	0	0	0

Entry mode	Host policy	Level of welfare	Firm size	Advert. industry	Knowl. industry	Resource industry	Activity 1	Activity 2	Activity 3	Activity 4	Activity 5	Activity 6
Minority JV	0.2981 (0.2891)	0.1328 (0.3469)	0.1810 (0.2813)	0.6041 (0.9755)	-0.5917 (0.8374)	-0.9952 (1.0788)	-5.9435* (.)	1.1528 (1.2244)	-2.3743** (1.2460)	-3.4958* (2.6330)	-8.4852* (.)	0.2147 (1.2452)
50/50 JV	-0.0965 (0.1550)	0.8805*** (0.3139)	-0.0426 (0.2514)	0.5016 (0.7500)	0.4324 (0.6053)	-0.7209 (0.8434)	0.0778 (1.8652)	-0.2986 (0.9457)	-1.7126** (0.8221)	-10.9633* (.)	-8.3647* (.)	-0.3777 (0.8353)
Majority JV	-0.2880** (0.1466)	0.5074* (0.2925)	-0.5443** (0.2408)	1.4155** (0.7549)	-0.1987 (0.6360)	-0.9621 (0.8314)	-6.1564* (.)	0.0473 (1.0523)	-1.6211* (0.8828)	-2.2687 (2.0583)	-8.5942* (.)	0.6221 (0.8977)
WOS	0	0	0	0	0	0	0	0	0	0	0	0

* $p < 0.1$; ** $p < 0.05$; *** $p < 0.01$ (one-tailed); ' infinite parameters, due to a lack of JVs involved in these activities. Values in parentheses are standard errors.
[1] A positive coefficient means an increased likelihood of the specific type of JV relative to a WOS.

5.5 Ordered logit analysis

Two ordered logit analyses were carried out: one with the division of equity as the criterion to classify JVs, and another with the division of control. The results of both models are presented in Table 5.10. Below, the results will be discussed.

Table 5.10 shows that a higher level of ownership is significantly more likely when the assets transferred to the new foreign subsidiary are highly specific ($p<0.05$), the level of competition is high ($p<0.01$), the foreign affiliate is relatively large ($p<0.01$), and the investing firm has a good reputation ($p<0.1$). When entry into developed countries is contemplated, lower levels of ownership are preferred ($p<0.1$). Furthermore, the U-shaped relationship between a lower level of ownership and cultural differences remains significant ($p<0.05$). All other variables turn out to have no significant impact on the level of ownership. Compared to the binomial and multinomial logit analyses, this ordered logit model reveals an insignificant effect of the riskiness of the host country, the firm's international and host country experience, and the growth of the industry entered. Apparently, no ordering exists among the four entry modes for these variables.

A remarkable difference between the results of the ordered logit model and the multinomial logit model concerns the outcome of the variable *asset specificity*. In the multinomial model, no significant effect was found for this variable on the likelihood of any of the three different types of JV, whereas the effect became significant at the 0.05 level in the ordered model. A closer look at Table 5.8 reveals that the estimated coefficients of the three types of JV (minority, 50/50, and majority) are ordered: -0.5702, -0.6885, and -1.0344, respectively. Hence, the multinomial logit model already contained indications of a possible significant effect of asset specificity on the ordering of the four entry modes.

When the level of control is taken as the criterion to categorize JVs, different results are obtained than in the case of the level of ownership. A higher level of control is preferred when competition in the industry entered is high ($p<0.05$), the investing firm has much international experience ($p<0.1$), and the relative size of the foreign investment is large ($p<0.05$). Lower control is preferred when the investing firm has much host country experience ($p<0.1$), and when risky countries ($p<0.05$) and developed countries ($p<0.05$) are entered (see Table 5.10). In addition, the U-shaped effect of cultural distance on the preference for a lower level of control is significant ($p<0.01$).

Table 5.10
Ordered logit estimations with JVs grouped on the level of equity and on the level of control[1]

Independent variables	Equity JV	Control JV
Intercept	2.7112*	1.4077
	(1.9165)	(1.9154)
Global strategy	-0.3621	-0.3489
	(0.3066)	(0.3038)
Level of competition	-0.4419***	-0.3498**
	(0.1536)	(0.1524)
Industry growth	0.1906	0.0939
	(0.1671)	(0.1656)
International experience	-0.4500	-0.7762*
	(0.5551)	(0.5532)
Host country experience	0.2670	0.5140*
	(0.3146)	(0.3224)
Product experience	0.0520	0.1298
	(0.1187)	(0.1236)
Relative size	-0.4167**	-0.3362**
	(0.1548)	(0.1528)
Asset specificity	-0.6995**	-0.5217
	(0.4098)	(0.4079)
Reputation	-0.1980*	-0.1730
	(0.1452)	(0.1448)
Cultural difference	-1.4926**	-1.7569***
	(0.7232)	(0.7283)
(Cultural difference)^2	0.3070**	0.3450***
	(0.1448)	(0.1458)
Host country risk	0.0943	0.1496**
	(0.0816)	(0.0816)
Host government policy	-0.0893	-0.0357
	(0.0990)	(0.1003)
Level of welfare	0.2422*	0.3034**
	(0.1650)	(0.1661)
Firm size	0.0026	0.0249
	(0.1392)	(0.1381)
Advertising-intensive industry	0.3806	0.4155
	(0.4674)	(0.4651)
Know-how-intensive industry	-0.2773	-0.1424
	(0.4009)	(0.4038)
Resource-intensive industry	-0.6565	-0.6573
	(0.5316)	(0.5372)
Type of activity (1)	0.6923	0.0410
	(1.4873)	(1.5005)
Type of activity (2)	0.1472	0.3870
	(0.6063)	(0.6047)
Type of activity (3)	-1.4295***	-1.4531***
	(0.5630)	(0.5615)
Type of activity (4)	-2.0061*	-2.5105**
	(1.3388)	(1.3384)
Type of activity (5)	-101.5000	-101.6000
	(2.98E21)	(2.90E21)
Type of activity (6)	-0.1565	-0.1669
	(0.5579)	(0.5559)
Model-χ^2	57.802	63.247
Significance	0.0001	0.0001
Degrees of freedom	24	24

* $p<0.1$; ** $p<0.05$; *** $p<0.01$ (one-tailed). Values in parentheses are standard errors.
[1] A positive coefficient means an increased likelihood of JVs.

A comparison of the two ordered logit analyses shows that three variables which had an insignificant coefficient in the model based on the division of equity are significant in the second model based on control. These variables are *international experience*, *host country experience*, and *host country risk*. Moreover, the two transactional variables (*asset specificity* and *reputation*), which significantly affect the preference of a high level of ownership, turn out to have no significant effect on the level of control. Apparently, only an increase in the level of ownership, and not in the level of control, can reduce the negative effects of opportunistic behaviour. This finding is in sharp contrast to the prediction of a number of authors using transaction cost economics, who argue that opportunistic behaviour (in the case of asset specificity or a good reputation) can best be prevented with a high *control* governance structure (see, e.g., Anderson and Gatignon, 1986; Hennart, 1988; Teece, 1986).

The criteria for the assessment of the overall fit of the two models indicate that both are good models: the -2LL's are 331.853 and 330.933, respectively, which are both insignificant. The model-χ^2's are 57.802 and 63.247, respectively, and highly significant (p<0.001). The ρ^2 of the two models is identical: 0.34. However, both models do not satisfy the requirement that they are invariant to the cutpoints. The two models are highly significant on the proportional odds assumption test: $\chi^2 = 134.5142$ with p<0.001, and $\chi^2 = 100.6691$ with p<0.001, respectively. This means that the coefficients of the explanatory variables are not independent of the mode of entry which is taken as the cutpoint (Menard, 1995). Thus, the coefficients shown in Table 5.10 will be different when 50/50 or majority JVs instead of minority JVs are taken as the cutpoint. This suggests that the four categories of the dependent variable (minority JV, 50/50 JV, majority JV, and WOS) really differ from one another, which is completely in line with the conclusion of the multinomial logit analyses (see section 5.4). The results (see Table 5.10), however, indicate that for some of the variables an ordering exists for the four types of entry mode.

The lack of invariance to the cutpoint implies that the results of the ordered logit analyses presented in Table 5.10 should be interpreted with care. The values of the coefficients of the independent variables should not be taken too literally, but more important is the level of significance and whether the effects are positive or negative.

5.6 Conclusions

At the end of this chapter, the three different types of logit models (binomial, multinomial, and ordered) are compared. In Table 5.11, the logit models are evaluated and compared following several criteria. The conclusion is that, based on the -2LL and the model-χ^2, all models are good models. However, these two criteria cannot be used to compare models with different assumptions, such as multinomial logit and ordered logit. Consequently, other criteria are used to compare the logit models.

Using the ρ^2 as the criterion for evaluation, it turns out that the two multinomial logit models are better than the other models. This is in line with the results of the different models, which provided clear evidence of the differences between the four entry modes. The conceptually plausible ordering of the four modes of entry (minority JV, 50/50 JV, majority JV, and WOS) is not corroborated by the data on Dutch foreign entries. Each mode turns out to have unique characteristics and, as a result, each type has its own circumstances in which it is the most appropriate mode of foreign entry. Therefore, there appears to be no real ordering between them, at least not for all variables. For a number of variables (six in the case of the division based on equity, and seven in the control-based division), the ordered logit analyses confirmed that an ordering exists among the four entry modes (minority JV, 50/50 JV, majority JV, and WOS).

The lack of ordering for all variables in combination with the larger number of variables with a significant effect on the entry mode choice (see Table 5.11) indicates that the multinomial logit models of this study better explain the foreign entry mode choice than the ordered logit models. This conclusion is in contradiction with the findings of Chu and Anderson (1992). They concluded that ordered logit models are more appropriate for foreign entry mode choices than unordered (i.e., multinomial) logit models.

The next chapter contains the conclusions and implications of this study.

Table 5.11
Comparison of the logit models: binomial, multinomial, and ordered

Evaluation criteria	Binomial logit	Multinomial logit equity	Multinomial logit control	Ordered logit equity	Ordered logit control
-2LL	159.965	263.655	277.523	331.853	330.933
Model-χ^2	71.066†	126.000†	116.654†	57.802†	63.247†
Degrees of freedom	24	69	69	24	24
ρ^2	0.31	0.43	0.40	0.35	0.34
Number of sign. indep. var.	10	11	11	6	7

† $p < 0.001$

Notes

1 These 206 non-responding firms represent approximately 77% of all firms that were phoned and did not respond (i.e., 266 firms), whereas the 112 responding firms constitute 68% of all 164 responding firms.

2 The number of degrees of freedom left is determined as follows: $((X * (X+1))/2) - n$; where X is the number of indicators and n stands for the number of parameters to be estimated. In the case of two indicators, the number of degrees of freedom is: $((2*3)/2) - (2+2) = -1$.

3 The correlation between these two indicators is only 0.347.

4 One-tailed significance levels are used since the hypotheses contain explicit predictions of the effect of the explanatory variables. One exception, however, is Hypothesis 14, in which the effect of the level of welfare is not specified. In this case, a two-tailed significance level is employed.

5 Compare Barkema, Bell, and Pennings (1996), who found that experience gained in cultural settings that are identical with or comparable to the host country's culture has a significant impact on the longevity of foreign majority JVs and foreign acquisitions. No such effect was identified for general international experience.

6 In developed countries, local firms are often MNEs themselves.

7 The overclassification of WOSs is much less than in previous studies (compare Hennart, 1991; Larimo, 1993).

8 Using the WOS as the base category implies that this study acknowledges that firms see the different JV types as real alternatives for WOSs. In other words, when entering a foreign market, firms are expected to make only one decision on the entry mode that will be

selected. This is in contrast to a so-called two-stage approach according to which firms first decide whether they want to enter by means of a JV or not, and in the second stage select the precise form of cooperation (Gatignon and Anderson, 1988).

6 Conclusions

In this last chapter, the conclusions of this study will be presented (section 6.1). These conclusions form the basis for the managerial implications, which are the subject of section 6.2. Finally, section 6.3 contains some suggestions for further research.

6.1 Conclusions

This study investigated the foreign entry mode choice. More precisely, it focused on what factors affect the choice between two specific entry modes: the JV and the WOS. The selection of the mode used to enter a foreign country is an important, though complex, strategic decision. Many factors influence this selection process. Therefore, it can be expected that many firms will have problems in determining the optimal mode of entry. Particularly, those firms that enter into cross-border activities for the first time will probably encounter many problems.

The research question of this study was:

What factors influence the choice between a JV and a WOS as the mode of foreign entry?

To gain insight into the possible impact of the factors that may be relevant for foreign entry mode choices, two trajectories were followed. First, the literature, both theoretical and empirical, was reviewed. Second, an empirical study was conducted to test the hypotheses that were formulated based on the literature review.

Seven theoretical approaches in the field of international business and strategic management were evaluated on their applicability to foreign entry mode choices: Hymer's market imperfections theory, transaction cost economics, internalization theory, Dunning's eclectic paradigm, the strategic behaviour approach, the resource-based approach, and the eclectic theory of the choice of the international entry mode by Hill, Hwang, and Kim (1990). All these theories turned out to be useful in explaining foreign entry mode choices. However, the focus in this study on the entry mode choice by individual firms necessitated that Hymer's market imperfections theory and Dunning's eclectic paradigm were omitted from the further analysis. Four of the remaining theories offer only partial explanations. Only Hill, Hwang, and Kim's eclectic theory was able to provide a more comprehensive framework for analysing foreign entry mode choices. This framework reflects the complexity and diversity of a firm's business environment much better than partial frameworks.

Hill, Hwang, and Kim's eclectic theory was taken as the starting point of the present study, as it combines elements of three relevant, complementary theoretical approaches: transaction cost economics, internalization theory, and the strategic behaviour approach. Various empirical studies found that elements of these theories significantly affect the choice between a JV and a WOS. In spite of its attractiveness, this eclectic theory was criticized in the present study. The main criticism concerns the neglect of the resource-based theory, which is one of the theories that provides a partial explanation of the foreign entry mode choice. This theory is oriented towards a firm's resources and capabilities. Given its focus and its level of analysis (i.e., the organizational unit), this approach is complementary to the strategic behaviour approach, internalization theory, and transaction cost economics. Furthermore, the relevance of this theory was empirically confirmed.

In the present study, Hill, Hwang, and Kim's eclectic framework was adjusted and extended, which resulted in a new eclectic framework. A major extension is that the resource-based theory is added to the framework. Hence, the present study's eclectic framework consists of elements of four theories: the strategic behaviour approach, the resource-based theory, transaction cost economics, and the internalization theory. This framework was used to formulate a number of hypotheses regarding the influence of strategic variables, ownership-specific variables, transactional variables, and locational variables on the choice between a JV and a WOS as the mode of entry.

A survey was held among Dutch MNEs which were expected to have set up one or more foreign JVs or foreign WOSs. The response to this survey resulted in a total number of 168 observations (73 JVs and 95 WOSs). Most explanatory variables were operationalized by several indicators to capture the complexity of these variables. In contrast to other studies, perceptual data were combined with archival data, since it was expected that both capture a different part of the variables. The data collected were firm-level data and venture-level data.

A two-step approach was followed to test the hypotheses. The first step consisted of estimating the measurement model using confirmatory factor analysis in LISREL. This means that it was investigated whether the indicators, which were expected to measure the explanatory variables, indeed measured these variables. All but two indicators turned out to be good measures of the latent variables. These two indicators were omitted from all further analyses. The output of this first step was used as the input for the second step: the testing of the hypotheses.

The hypotheses were tested using three different types of logit models: binomial logit, multinomial logit, and ordered logit. In the binomial logit model, the dependent variable was either a JV or a WOS. The results of this logit analysis clearly showed that the eclectic framework that was developed in this study is not only conceptually, but also empirically superior to partial and less comprehensive models. Nevertheless, the partial models (i.e., based on only one theory) and the less comprehensive models (i.e., based on two or three of the relevant theories) in themselves also were good models.

According to the binomial logit analysis, JVs are more likely to be established when a high-growth industry is entered, the investing firm has much host country experience, the cultural differences between the home and the host country are either very small or very large, a risky host country is entered, and the host country has a high level of welfare. JVs are less likely, or, put differently, WOSs are more likely, to be established when the level of competition in the industry entered is high, the investing firm has much international experience, the size of the foreign subsidiary is relatively large, the assets transferred to the foreign affiliate are highly specific, and the investing firm has a good reputation. Three variables (the investing firm's strategy, its experience with the products, and the policy of the host government) appeared to have no significant effect on the choice between a JV and a WOS.

These results concerning individual effects are to a large extent comparable to the findings of previous studies (see Table 2.1). Five variables turned out to have effects which deviated from earlier findings:

1 The level of competition has a negative effect on JVs, whereas previous studies found a positive effect (Gomes-Casseres, 1990) or no effect at all (Hennart, 1991; Kogut and Singh, 1988b; Larimo, 1993).

2   The experience with the host country has a positive effect on JVs, whereas earlier research (Gomes-Casseres, 1989, 1990; Hennart, 1991; Padmanabhan and Cho, 1994) found the opposite.
3   The relative size of the foreign subsidiary turned out to have a negative effect on the likelihood of JVs, whereas former studies showed a positive effect (Kogut and Singh, 1988b) or an insignificant effect (Hennart, 1991; Larimo, 1993).
4   A U-shaped relationship between cultural differences and JVs was confirmed. So far, only linear positive (Agarwal, 1994; Agarwal and Ramaswami, 1992b; Benito, 1996; Erramilli, 1991; Erramilli and Rao, 1993; Gatignon and Anderson, 1988) and linear negative (Madhok, 1994; Padmanabhan and Cho, 1994) effects or insignificant effects (Larimo, 1993) were found.
5   In the present study, host government policy did not affect the choice between a JV and a WOS. Studies that investigated less recently established foreign entries provided significant support for an increased likelihood of JVs (Gatignon and Anderson, 1988; Gomes-Casseres, 1989, 1990; Padmanabhan and Cho, 1994; Shane, 1993).

Nevertheless, most variables appear to affect the entry mode choice in the same way as in previous studies. This comparison with previous studies indicates that the different way of measuring the variables that is employed in this study (viz., multiple indicators, subjective data and archival data, firm-level and venture-level data, Dutch foreign entries) does not lead to very different results. For most variables, the effect seems robust for the precise way in which it is measured.

Two different multinomial logit models were estimated. The first was based on the division of equity as the criterion for classifying JVs into minority-, 50/50-, and majority-owned JVs. In the second model, the division of control was used as the criterion. The results of both models, which are largely comparable to the results of the binomial logit model, showed manifestly that JVs should not be regarded as one group of organizational forms. In contrast, there are many differences among minority JVs, 50/50 JVs, and majority JVs!!! Furthermore, the multinomial logit analyses revealed that differences exist between the classification of JVs on equity and control. Minority-owned JVs, for example, turn out to be not always identical to minority-controlled JVs.

The last type of logit analysis concerns the ordered logit model. In this model, it is assumed that the categories of the dependent variable are ordinal. Analogous to the multinomial logit model, two different orders are distinguished: one based on the level of equity and one based on the level of control. The results of the two models indicate that the models are not invariant to the cutpoints, which implies that the coefficients of the explanatory variables are not independent from the mode of entry which is taken as the cutpoint. This suggests that the four categories of the dependent variable (minority JV, 50/50 JV, majority JV, and WOS) really differ from one another, which is completely in line with the conclusion of the multinomial logit analyses. The results, however, indicate that for some of the variables an ordering exists for the four types of entry mode (see Table 5.10).

In sum, the eclectic framework that was developed in this study turned out to be not only conceptually, but also empirically superior to partial and less comprehensive models. The methodology used proved to be fruitful for capturing the complexities that are predominantly present in foreign entry mode choices. A final conclusion is that minority JVs, 50/50 JVs, and majority JVs should not be regarded as one group of JVs: they are genuinely different forms of organization.

6.2 Implications of the results

This section contains some 'translations' of the results to the practice of decision makers. An attempt will be made to indicate what the implications of both the framework and the results are for decision makers who are responsible for selecting the appropriate mode of foreign entry.

Apart from choosing the country in which to enter, a firm has to choose the mode of entry. The choice of the entry mode is a crucial decision, which may determine the success or failure of the entry. In some situations, the wrong choice may even threaten the survival of the firm. Therefore, it is of the utmost importance to invest time and money in investigating and evaluating as many relevant variables as possible before the choice of entry mode is made. The eclectic framework developed in this study is a useful instrument for selecting the right mode of entry.

Every situation is unique. Therefore, the framework cannot be used without making the necessary adjustments for the particular situation. Firms should try to concentrate most of their attention on the variables that are most relevant for their situation, and divide the remaining time over the less relevant ones. A further aspect that should not be disregarded is that some of the variables which were not supported by the empirical data may turn out to be relevant in individual settings. For example, when a firm actually pursues a global strategy, it is critical that all, or almost all, activities are coordinated centrally. In such a case, the need for full control may be more pressing than in other circumstances.

The variables incorporated in the eclectic framework should not be considered on their own; their impact should be evaluated in conjunction with the other variables. Depending on its specific situation, a firm may opt for a WOS as the mode of entry in a culturally distant country, because it has much international experience. This example illustrates that all relevant variables should be considered jointly, whereby possible JV-encouraging aspects may be neutralized by WOS-encouraging aspects.

When using the outcomes of this study, firms should always keep in mind their limitations and the constraints imposed by stakeholders. For example, a firm that wishes to set up a relatively large WOS but does not possess sufficient financial resources to establish the subsidiary on its own, is forced to select a different mode of entry, or withdraw its plan to invest.

A final important issue is that the intuition of decision makers is vital in choosing the right entry mode. This holds particularly for situations in which it is not possible to consider and evaluate all relevant variables. However, intuition should not be the only basis for the selection of an entry mode. Attempts to systematically detect the most decisive aspects in the firm's environment remain important. This not only forces decision makers to rethink their process of decision making critically, but also facilitates the evaluation of the choice made. Only then, firms can learn from their previous decisions and choices.

6.3 Suggestions for further research

Like all studies, the present study has a limited scope. One can think of many issues that are also interesting to investigate, but that are beyond the scope of this study. As such, they can be labelled the limitations of the study. In this final section, these issues are presented as suggestions for further research. Five paths for additional research are proposed.

First, the present study used a static approach, which, by definition, only gives insight into the situation at one moment in time. Of course, the firm's environment is a dynamic setting characterized by many changes and developments. For instance, risky countries can become less risky over time, and vice versa. In addition, firms may also learn from their experiences, which may affect their way of perceiving the (developments in the) environment. These dynamic aspects are largely ignored when taking a static approach.

To incorporate more dynamism into a study on foreign entry mode choices, more elements should be borrowed from dynamic approaches such as the internationalization process model or Uppsala model (see, e.g., Johanson and Vahlne, 1977, 1990; Johanson and Wiedersheim-Paul, 1975), the innovation-adoption-inspired internationalization models (Andersen, 1993; Bilkey and Tesar, 1977; Cavusgil, 1980), and the product cycle model (Melin, 1992; Vernon, 1966, 1979). Particularly the internationalization process model, which considers the internationalization of a firm to be an incremental learning process, has been frequently corroborated in empirical studies (see, e.g., Bilkey, 1978; Bilkey and Tesar, 1977; Cavusgil, 1980, 1982; Czinkota, 1982; Davidson, 1980, 1983; Denis and Depelteau, 1985; Ford et al., 1987; Johanson and Wiedersheim-Paul, 1975; Luostarinen, 1980; Newbould, Buckley, and Thurwell, 1978; Tschoegl, 1982). However, in more recent empirical studies, the Uppsala model was not supported (see, e.g., Benito and Gripsrud, 1992; Engwall and Wallenstål, 1988; Hedlund and Kverneland, 1985, 1986; Johanson and Sharma, 1987; Nordström, 1991; Sullivan and Bauerschmidt, 1990; Turnbull, 1987). This suggests that this dynamic model is especially germane in the early stages of internationalization (Johanson and Vahlne, 1990; Melin, 1992). Irrespective of the mixed support for the dynamic internationalization process approach, it remains interesting to incorporate more dynamic elements in a study on foreign entry mode choices. Longitudinal studies rather than cross-sectional studies are required to capture the dynamism.

A second suggestion for further research is to attempt to examine the role and influence of *intuition*. In general, static approaches implicitly assume that decision makers are able to evaluate the effects of all possibly relevant variables rationally. Such an evaluation is very complex, since hardly quantifiable, hardly predictable, and sometimes even contradictory effects have to be included. In practice, however, most decision makers are not hyperrational. Hence, they partially base their decisions on their intuitions. So far, the influence of intuition has received too little attention in the literature on foreign entry mode choices. In-depth interviews with decision makers and in-depth case studies may provide more insight into the balance between ratio and intuition in foreign entry mode choices.

Third, the present study only focused on the *incidence* of JVs and WOSs. Therefore, nothing can be said about the best mode of entry in terms of *success*. One might say that the most successful mode of entry will most likely be chosen by decision makers. However, this statement supposes that decision makers are hyperrational. The questionnaire used in this study contained one question on the success of the foreign venture. Most of the respondents (61.9 per cent) indicated that they were satisfied with the performance of the foreign subsidiary, whereas only 7.1 per cent was dissatisfied.[1] For the remaining foreign entries no opinion could be given yet, since they were still in the initial phase. The low percentage of failure and the high percentage of 'unknowns' makes that no conclusions can be drawn about the success and failure of the foreign ventures. Therefore, in line with recent research (see Barkema, Bell, and Pennings, 1996; Blodgett, 1992; Li, 1995; Woodcock, Beamish, and Makino, 1994), more research needs to be done to gain insight into the precise impact of variables on the success and failure of foreign entries.

As described in Chapter 2, many different modes of entry can be distinguished. The fourth suggestion involves the use of the eclectic framework developed for analysing and testing the choice of entry modes other than JV or WOS. Possibly, the framework needs to be adapted because of the specific characteristics of the various entry modes.

Finally, it may be worthwhile to employ and test the eclectic framework of this study in different settings, such as product-market entries and regional-market entries. Furthermore, the foreign entry mode choice of firms from one or more different home countries may be examined using this eclectic framework. Then, possible country-of-origin effects can be filtered out.

Note

1   These scores were 53.3 per cent and 9.3 per cent for JVs, and 68.8 per cent and 5.4 per cent for WOSs, respectively.

Appendix A Questionnaire

QUESTIONNAIRE

The aim of this questionnaire is to gain insight into the choice of foreign entry mode. In the present study, two possible entry modes are distinguished: joint ventures and wholly owned subsidiaries. For both modes comparable questions are included.

The questionnaire consists of three separate parts:
I   Introduction and definitions
II General questions
III Specific questions

The first part explains the way in which to fill in the questionnaire, and provides definitions of important terms. Next, some general questions on your firm will be posed. The third part contains a number of questions related to the two modes of foreign entry.

I Introduction and definition

Please read this introduction carefully before filling in the questionnaire!!!

The **general** questions concern the firm, division, or business unit where you are currently working. Depending on your position, references to the term 'firm' should be replaced by either 'division' or 'business unit'. Please answer the questions from the perspective of the entity where you hold your position.

The **specific** questions involve a foreign entry with a joint venture and a wholly owned subsidiary. Please take notice of the following directions when answering the questions:

1. Think of a recent foreign joint venture the establishment of which you were personally involved in.
2. Subsequently, answer the specific questions on joint ventures.
3. Do the same for a recently established wholly owned subsidiary.

Please fill in the questionnaire for both modes of entry. If it is impossible for you to do so, please answer the questions for the mode of entry in which you and your firm were involved. The questionnaire contains questions with a 7-point scale. Please circle the number that is most in line with reality.

Example: Suppose that the following question is asked: 'How was the economic situation in the host country when your firm entered that country?'. The answer categories possible range from 'very good' to 'very bad'.

---

very good   7   6   5   4   3   2   1   very bad

If the host country's economic situation was very good, number '7' should be circled. Analogously, number '1' should be circled if the situation was very bad. If the economic situation can be characterized as somewhere between very good and very bad, the number which best represents the economic situation should be chosen. In case questions are not relevant to your firm/division/business unit, write down 'irrelevant'.

For the sake of clarity, the two modes of entry are defined as follows:

Joint venture: A form of partial cooperation between two or more firms, whereby the partners have a stake in the newly established entity and, in theory, are able to influence the decisions of this new entity. Cooperation is only partial because not all the activities of the partners are involved in the cooperation.

Wholly owned subsidiary: A (daughter) firm set up from scratch by one firm, the latter being the only firm that is in the position to influence the decisions of the former.

II General questions

The general questions involve your firm/division/business unit, dependent on your position (see Introduction).

Name firm/division/business unit:
Core activities:
Number of **employees**:
Sales in 1992:
Ratio equity/total assets:

1. *How much **experience** does your firm have with international operations?*

   | very much | 7 | 6 | 5 | 4 | 3 | 2 | 1 | none |

2. ***How many** foreign joint ventures and/or wholly owned subsidiaries does your firm have?*

   - ☐ 0 (You may stop here!)
   - ☐ 1 - 10
   - ☐ 11 - 25
   - ☐ 26 - 50
   - ☐ more than 50

3. ***When** did your firm set up its **first** foreign joint venture or foreign wholly owned subsidiary?*

   - ☐ before 1920
   - ☐ 1920 - 1945
   - ☐ 1946 - 1980
   - ☐ after 1980

4. *What **appreciation** do **your clients** have for your firm as compared to its competitors?*

   very high   7   6   5   4   3   2   1   very low

5. *Does your firm invest much money in its **image** (e.g., brand name, quality image) as compared to competing firms?*

   very much   7   6   5   4   3   2   1   nothing

6. a. *Does your firm have an a-priori **preference** for a specific entry mode?*

   ☐ yes
   ☐ no

   b. *If so, please indicate the **sequence** of preferences. (Please write down 1 to the entry mode which is preferred most, a 2 to the mode which is subsequently preferred, and so on.)*

   ☐ joint venture
   ☐ wholly owned subsidiary
   ☐ another mode, viz.:

   c. *Please **explain** this sequence of preferences.*

III Specific questions

The following questions deal with the entry modes:
A joint venture   (questions 7-36);
B wholly owned subsidiary (questions 37-63).

A: JOINT VENTURE

When answering the questions, please think of a foreign joint venture which was recently established by your firm/division/business unit to enter a foreign market.

7. *Name of joint venture (A):*

8. *Host country (X):*

9. a. *Year of actual **establishment**:* ....

    b. *Year of **dissolution**:*

    ☐ 19..
    ☐ still in operation

Core activities:

10. *What is the **core activity** of joint venture (A)?*

11. *To what extent does the **core activity** of joint venture (A) differ from the **core activities** of your firm?*

    | very much | 7 | 6 | 5 | 4 | 3 | 2 | 1 | not |

12. *What **type of activities** are carried out within joint venture (A)?*
    (More answers are possible!)

☐	research and development
☐	production
☐	marketing and sales
☐	other, viz.

Each product has a so-called **life-cycle**. This life-cycle can be divided into four separate stages: introduction, expansion, maturity, and decline. The introduction stage concerns the period in which a product is introduced to the market. In the expansion stage, the sales of the product increase substantially. Then, the speed of the increase decreases because of saturation of the market (maturity stage). Finally, the demand for the product will become negative (i.e., the decline stage). Two different life-cycles can be distinguished: (1) a life-cycle which focuses on the sales in **the Netherlands**; and (2) a life-cycle based on **foreign** demand. In question 13, these life-cycles are called the **'domestic'** and the **'foreign'** life-cycle, respectively.

13. a. *Into what **stage** of the **'domestic'** life-cycle could the core activity of joint venture (A) be classified at the time of establishing joint venture (A)?*

☐	introduction
☐	expansion
☐	maturity
☐	decline

    b. *Into what **stage** of the **'foreign'** life-cycle could the core activity of joint venture (A) be classified at the time of establishing joint venture (A)?*

☐	introduction
☐	expansion
☐	maturity
☐	decline

Relationship:

14. *How many **other firms** were involved in joint venture (A)?*

    ☐ 1
    ☐ 2
    ☐ 3
    ☐ more than 3

15. *What is the **equity** division of joint venture (A)?*

    your firm: .... %
    partner 1:   .... %
    partner 2:   .... %
    other partners: .... %

16. *How much **actual control** does your firm have over joint venture (A)?*

    ☐ majority
    ☐ as much as the partner (<u>only</u> in the case of one partner)
    ☐ minority

Experience:

17. a. *Did your firm engage in **one or more foreign joint ventures** before joint venture (A) was set up?*

    ☐ yes
    ☐ no (please continue with question 18)

b. *What was, in general, your **experience** with these joint ventures?*

| very good | 7 | 6 | 5 | 4 | 3 | 2 | 1 | very bad |

c. *Please **explain**.*

_____
_____
_____

18. *How familiar was your firm with the **characteristics** of country (X) (e.g., customer needs, market structure, culture, the division of power, the attitude towards foreign firms), before joint venture (A) was set up?*

| very | 7 | 6 | 5 | 4 | 3 | 2 | 1 | not |

19. a. *How much **experience** did your firm have in operating in country (X) before joint venture (A) was set up?*

| very much | 7 | 6 | 5 | 4 | 3 | 2 | 1 | none |

b. *What was your firm's **reputation** in country (X) before joint venture (A) was set up?*

| very good | 7 | 6 | 5 | 4 | 3 | 2 | 1 | very bad |

c. *What was your firm's **reputation** in the **industry entered** before joint venture (A) was set up?*

| very good | 7 | 6 | 5 | 4 | 3 | 2 | 1 | very bad |

Input:

20. a. *How much **technological know how** that <u>only your firm</u> possesses did your firm contribute to joint venture (A)?*

| very much | 7 | 6 | 5 | 4 | 3 | 2 | 1 | nothing |

b. *How great was the **risk** that other firms would profit from, or even abuse, this unique know-how?*

| very great | 7 | 6 | 5 | 4 | 3 | 2 | 1 | very small |

21. a. *How many **skills** (such as management techniques, process control, quality control, marketing know-how) that <u>only your firm</u> possesses did your firm contribute to joint venture (A)?*

| very many | 7 | 6 | 5 | 4 | 3 | 2 | 1 | nothing |

b. *How great was the **risk** that other firms would profit from, or even abuse, these unique skills?*

| very great | 7 | 6 | 5 | 4 | 3 | 2 | 1 | very small |

22. a. *How many **natural resources** (such as oil, wood, ore, coal, rubber) from country (X) did joint venture (A) use?*

| very many | 7 | 6 | 5 | 4 | 3 | 2 | 1 | nothing |

b. *To what extent were the natural resources used by joint venture (A) **easily available**?*

| very easily | 7 | 6 | 5 | 4 | 3 | 2 | 1 | not easily |

Financial aspects:

23. *Did your firm have many **financial resources** at the time of establishing joint venture (A)?*

| very many | 7 | 6 | 5 | 4 | 3 | 2 | 1 | none |

24. *What is the **relative size** (measured in invested capital) of joint venture (A) compared to your firm?*

| very large | 7 | 6 | 5 | 4 | 3 | 2 | 1 | very small |

25. a. *Is the output (the products) of joint venture (A) sold **solely in country (X)**?*

☐ yes
☐ no

b. *What part of the sales of joint venture (A) is sold to **other divisions/business units** of your firm?*

☐ nothing
☐ a minor part (less than 10%)
☐ a major part (10% or more)

26. a. *What was the **annual growth in sales** of the **industry** entered at the time of establishing joint venture (A)?*

| strongly positive | 7 | 6 | 5 | 4 | 3 | 2 | 1 | strongly negative |

b. *What was the **chance** of continuation of this sales growth?*

| very large | 7 | 6 | 5 | 4 | 3 | 2 | 1 | very small |

Characteristics of country (X):

27. *What was the **political** stability of country (X) at the time of establishing joint venture (A)?*

| very good | 7 | 6 | 5 | 4 | 3 | 2 | 1 | very bad |

28. *What was the **economic** situation in country (X) at the time of establishing joint venture (A)?*

| very good | 7 | 6 | 5 | 4 | 3 | 2 | 1 | very bad |

29. *How large were the **remaining risks** (such as the likelihood of natural disasters, crop failure, strikes, and so on) related to investing **in country (X)** at the time of establishing joint venture (A)?*

| very large | 7 | 6 | 5 | 4 | 3 | 2 | 1 | very small |

30. *To what extent were there **cultural differences** (e.g., with regard to norms, values, customs, relationships with people) between country (X) and your firm at the time of establishing joint venture (A)?*

| very many | 7 | 6 | 5 | 4 | 3 | 2 | 1 | none |

31. *How many **restrictions** (e.g., limitation of the percentage of ownership your firm could have, meeting local requirements) did the government of country (X) impose upon your firm?*

| very many | 7 | 6 | 5 | 4 | 3 | 2 | 1 | none |

32. a. *To what extent did the **government of country (X) stimulate** (e.g., by means of tax holidays, market protection, subsidies, low-interest loans) your firm to cooperate with a local firm?*

| very much | 7 | 6 | 5 | 4 | 3 | 2 | 1 | not at all |

b. *To what extent did the **Dutch government stimulate** your firm to choose a joint venture as the mode of entry?*

| very much | 7 | 6 | 5 | 4 | 3 | 2 | 1 | not at all |

33. *To what extent were local firms in country (X) **attractive** regarding their level of knowledge and education?*

| very much | 7 | 6 | 5 | 4 | 3 | 2 | 1 | not at all |

Competition:

34. *How many **potential competitors** were present in the industry entered at the time of establishing joint venture (A)?*

| very many | 7 | 6 | 5 | 4 | 3 | 2 | 1 | none |

35. a. *What was the **intensity of competition** in the industry entered at the time of establishing joint venture (A)?*

| very high | 7 | 6 | 5 | 4 | 3 | 2 | 1 | very low |

b. *To what extent did a previous **entry of a competitor** in country (X) influence the **entry** of your firm?*

| very much | 7 | 6 | 5 | 4 | 3 | 2 | 1 | not at all |

c. *To what extent did a previous **entry of a competitor** in country (X) influence the **entry mode choice** of your firm?*

| very much | 7 | 6 | 5 | 4 | 3 | 2 | 1 | not at all |

Success/failure:

36. a. *Are you satisfied with the performance of joint venture (A), or, stated differently, do you consider joint venture (A)* **successful***?*

    ☐ yes
    ☐ no
    ☐ cannot be assessed yet
    ☐ other, viz.:

    b. *Please **explain**.*

Please write down below any remarks you may have about joint venture (A), country (X) or the questionnaire:

B: WHOLLY OWNED SUBSIDIARY

When answering the questions, please think of a foreign wholly owned subsidiary which was recently established by your firm/division/ business unit to enter a foreign market.

37. **Name** of wholly owned subsidiary **(B)**:

38. **Host country (Y)**:

39. a. Year of actual **establishment**:   ....

   b. Year of **dissolution**:

☐	19..
☐	still in operation

Core activities:

40. What is the **core activity** of wholly owned subsidiary (B)?

41. To what extent does the **core activity** of wholly owned subsidiary (B) differ from the **core activities** of your firm?

very much	7	6	5	4	3	2	1	not

42. What **type of activities** are carried out within wholly owned subsidiary (B)? (*More answers are possible!*)

☐	research and development
☐	production
☐	marketing and sales
☐	other, viz.

Each product has a so-called **life-cycle**. This life-cycle can be divided into four separate stages: introduction, expansion, maturity, and decline. The introduction stage concerns the period in which a product is introduced to the market. In the expansion stage, the sales of the product increase substantially. Then, the speed of the increase decreases because of saturation of the market (maturity stage). Finally, the demand for the product will become negative (i.e., the decline stage). Two different life-cycles can be distinguished: (1) a life-cycle which focuses on the sales in **the Netherlands**; and (2) a life-cycle based on **foreign** demand. In question 43, these life-cycles are called the **'domestic'** and the **'foreign'** life-cycle, respectively.

43. a. *Into what **stage** of the **'domestic'** life-cycle could the core activity of wholly owned subsidiary (B) be classified at the time of establishing wholly owned subsidiary (B)?*

    ☐ introduction
    ☐ expansion
    ☐ maturity
    ☐ decline

    b. *Into what **stage** of the **'foreign'** life-cycle could the core activity of wholly owned subsidiary (B) be classified at the time of establishing wholly owned subsidiary (B)?*

    ☐ introduction
    ☐ expansion
    ☐ maturity
    ☐ decline

Experience:

44. a. *Did your firm engage in **one or more foreign wholly owned subsidiaries** before wholly owned subsidiary (B) was set up?*

    ☐ yes
    ☐ no (please continue with question 45)

b. *What was, in general, your **experience** with these wholly owned subsidiaries?*

| very good | 7 | 6 | 5 | 4 | 3 | 2 | 1 | very bad |

c. *Please **explain**.*

_____

_____

_____

45. *How familiar was your firm with the **characteristics** of country (Y) (e.g., customer needs, market structure, culture, the division of power, the attitude towards foreign firms), before wholly owned subsidiary (B) was set up?*

| very | 7 | 6 | 5 | 4 | 3 | 2 | 1 | not |

46. a. *How much **experience** did your firm have in operating in **country (Y)** before wholly owned subsidiary (B) was set up?*

| very much | 7 | 6 | 5 | 4 | 3 | 2 | 1 | none |

b. *What was your firm's **reputation** in **country (Y)** before wholly owned subsidiary (B) was set up?*

| very good | 7 | 6 | 5 | 4 | 3 | 2 | 1 | very bad |

c. *What was your firm's **reputation** in the **industry entered** before wholly owned subsidiary (B) was set up?*

| very good | 7 | 6 | 5 | 4 | 3 | 2 | 1 | very bad |

Input:

47. a. *How much **technological know how** that <u>only your firm</u> possesses did your firm contribute to wholly owned subsidiary (B)?*

    | very much | 7 | 6 | 5 | 4 | 3 | 2 | 1 | nothing |

    b. *How great was the **risk** that other firms would profit from, or even abuse, this unique know-how?*

    | very great | 7 | 6 | 5 | 4 | 3 | 2 | 1 | very small |

48. a. *How many **skills** (such as management techniques, process control, quality control, marketing know-how) that <u>only your firm</u> possesses did your firm contribute to wholly owned subsidiary (B)?*

    | very many | 7 | 6 | 5 | 4 | 3 | 2 | 1 | nothing |

    b. *How great was the **risk** that other firms would profit from, or even abuse, these unique skills?*

    | very great | 7 | 6 | 5 | 4 | 3 | 2 | 1 | very small |

49. a. *How many **natural resources** (such as oil, wood, ore, coal, rubber) from country (Y) did wholly owned subsidiary (B) use?*

    | very many | 7 | 6 | 5 | 4 | 3 | 2 | 1 | nothing |

    b. *To what extent were the natural resources used by wholly owned subsidiary (B) **easily available**?*

    | very easily | 7 | 6 | 5 | 4 | 3 | 2 | 1 | not easily |

Financial aspects:

50. *Did your firm have many **financial resources** at the time of establishing wholly owned subsidiary (B)?*

    | very many | 7 | 6 | 5 | 4 | 3 | 2 | 1 | none |

51. *What is the **relative size** (measured in invested capital) of wholly owned subsidiary (B) compared to your firm?*

    | very large | 7 | 6 | 5 | 4 | 3 | 2 | 1 | very small |

52. a. *Is the output (the products) of wholly owned subsidiary (B) sold **solely in country (Y)**?*

    ☐ yes
    ☐ no

    b. *What part of the sales of wholly owned subsidiary (B) is sold to **other divisions/business units** of your firm?*

    ☐ nothing
    ☐ a minor part (less than 10%)
    ☐ a major part (10% or more)

53. a. *What was the **annual growth in sales** of the **industry** entered at the time of establishing wholly owned subsidiary (B)?*

    | strongly positive | 7 | 6 | 5 | 4 | 3 | 2 | 1 | strongly negative |

    b. *What was the **chance** of continuation of this sales growth?*

    | very large | 7 | 6 | 5 | 4 | 3 | 2 | 1 | very small |

Characteristics of country (Y):

54. *What was the **political** stability of country (Y) at the time of establishing wholly owned subsidiary (B)?*

| very good | 7 | 6 | 5 | 4 | 3 | 2 | 1 | very bad |

55. *What was the **economic** situation in country (Y) at the time of establishing wholly owned subsidiary (B)?*

| very good | 7 | 6 | 5 | 4 | 3 | 2 | 1 | very bad |

56. *How large were the **remaining risks** (e.g., the likelihood of natural disasters, crop failure, strikes, and so on) related to investing in country (Y) at the time of establishing wholly owned subsidiary (B)?*

| very large | 7 | 6 | 5 | 4 | 3 | 2 | 1 | very small |

57. *To what extent were there **cultural differences** (e.g., with regard to norms, values, relationships with people) between country (Y) and your firm at the time of establishing wholly owned subsidiary (B)?*

| very many | 7 | 6 | 5 | 4 | 3 | 2 | 1 | none |

58. *How many **restrictions** (e.g., limitation of the percentage of ownership your firm could have, meeting local requirements) did the government of country (Y) impose upon your firm?*

| very many | 7 | 6 | 5 | 4 | 3 | 2 | 1 | none |

59. a. *To what extent did the **government of country (Y) stimulate** (e.g., by means of tax holidays, market protection, subsidies, low-interest loans) your firm to cooperate with a local firm?*

| very much | 7 | 6 | 5 | 4 | 3 | 2 | 1 | not at all |

b. *To what extent did the **Dutch government stimulate** your firm to choose a wholly owned subsidiary as the mode of entry?*

| very much | 7 | 6 | 5 | 4 | 3 | 2 | 1 | not at all |

60. *To what extent were local firms in country (Y) **attractive** regarding their level of knowledge and education?*

| very much | 7 | 6 | 5 | 4 | 3 | 2 | 1 | not at all |

Competition:

61. *How many **potential competitors** were present in the industry entered at the time of establishing wholly owned subsidiary (B)?*

| very many | 7 | 6 | 5 | 4 | 3 | 2 | 1 | none |

62. a. *What was the **intensity of competition** in the industry entered at the time of establishing wholly owned subsidiary (B)?*

| very high | 7 | 6 | 5 | 4 | 3 | 2 | 1 | very low |

b. *To what extent did a previous **entry of a competitor** in country (Y) influence the **entry** of your firm?*

| very much | 7 | 6 | 5 | 4 | 3 | 2 | 1 | not at all |

c. *To what extent did a previous **entry of a competitor** in country (Y) influence the **entry mode choice** of your firm?*

| very much | 7 | 6 | 5 | 4 | 3 | 2 | 1 | not at all |

Success/failure:

63. a. *Are you satisfied with the performance of wholly owned subsidiary (B), or, stated differently, do you consider wholly owned subsidiary (B) **successful**?*

    ☐ yes
    ☐ no
    ☐ cannot be assessed yet
    ☐ other, viz.:

   b. *Please **explain**.*

Please write down below any remarks you may have about wholly owned subsidiary (B), country (Y) or the questionnaire:

Appendix B
List of host countries

The following host countries were entered by the Dutch firms included in the survey:[1]

Argentina	Malaysia
Austria	Malta
Belgium	Namibia
Canada	Netherlands Antilles
Chile	Nigeria
China	Norway
Czech Republic	Poland
Denmark	Portugal
Estonia	Romania
France	Saudi Arabia
Germany	Singapore
Greece	Spain
Hong Kong	Sweden
Hungary	Syria
India	Taiwan
Indonesia	Thailand
Ireland	Turkey
Italy	United Kingdom
Japan	USA
Korea	Yemen

[1] For eleven entries, the host country was unknown.

List of references

Agarwal, S. 1994. Socio-cultural distance and the choice of joint ventures: A contingency perspective. *Journal of International Marketing*, 2(2): 63-80.

Agarwal, S. & S.N. Ramaswami. 1992a. Choice of foreign market entry mode: Impact of ownership, location and internalization factors. *Journal of International Business Studies*, 23(1): 1-27.

Agarwal, S. & S.N. Ramaswami. 1992b. *Choice of organizational form in foreign markets: A transaction cost perspective.* Paper presented at the 1992 AIB Annual Meeting in Brussels.

Aharoni, Y. 1966. *The foreign investment decision process.* Boston: Harvard Business School.

Aldrich, J.H. & F.D. Nelson. 1984. *Linear probability, logit, and probit models.* Sage University Paper Series on Quantitative Applications in the Social Sciences, 07-045. Beverly Hills, CA: Sage Publications.

Aliber, R.Z. 1970. A theory of direct foreign investment. In C.P. Kindleberger (ed.). *The international corporation.* Cambridge, MA: MIT Press.

Amemiya, T. 1981. Qualitative response models: A survey. *Journal of Economic Literature*, XIX(December): 1483-1536.

Amit, R. & P.J. Schoemaker. 1993. Strategic assets and organizational rent. *Strategic Management Journal*, 14(1): 33-46.

Andersen, O. 1993. On the internationalization process of firms: A critical analysis. *Journal of International Business Studies*, 24(2): 209-231.

Anderson, E. & H. Gatignon. 1986. Modes of foreign entry: A transaction cost analysis and propositions. *Journal of International Business Studies*, 17(2): 1-26.

Anderson, J.C. & D.W. Gerbing. 1988. Structural equation modeling in practice: A review and recommended two-step approach. *Psychological Bulletin*, 103: 411-423.

Anderson, J.C. & D.W. Gerbing. 1992. Assumptions and comparative strenghts of the two-step approach: Comment on Fornell and Yi. *Sociological Methods & Research*, 20(3): 321-333.

Ansoff, I. 1965. *Corporate strategy*. Harmondsworth: Penguin Books.

Babbie, E. 1990. *Survey research methods*. 2nd. ed. Belmont, CA: Wadsworth Publishing Company.

Backhaus, K., B. Erichson, W. Plinke, C. Schuchard-Ficher & R. Weiber. 1987. *Multivariate analysemethoden: Eine anwendungsorientierte einfuhrung*. 4th. ed. Berlin: Springer-Verlag.

Bain, J.S. 1956. *Barriers to new competition*. Cambridge, MA: Harvard University Press.

Banks, G. 1983. The economics and politics of countertrade. *The World Economy*, 6: 159-182.

Barkema, H.G., J.H.J. Bell & J.M. Pennings. 1996. Foreign entry, cultural barriers, and learning. *Strategic Management Journal*, 17: 151-166.

Barney, J.B. 1986. Strategic factor markets: Expectations, luck, and business strategy. *Management Science*, (October): 1231-1241.

Bartlett, C.A. & S. Ghoshal. 1989. *Managing across borders: The transnational solution*. London: Hutchinson Business Books.

Beamish, P.W. & J.C. Banks. 1987. Equity joint ventures and the theory of the multinational enterprise. *Journal of International Business Studies*, 18(3): 1-16.

Bell, J.H.J. 1993a. International joint ventures versus greenfield investments: A comprehensive approach. In A.M. Rugman & A. Verbeke (eds.). *Research in global strategic management: Beyond Porter*. Greenwich, CT: JAI Press, 199-220.

Bell, J.H.J. 1993b. Joint ventures: Succes en falen [Joint ventures: Success and failure]. In P. Duffhues, J. Groeneveld & J. Ooninckx (eds.). *Financiële Leiding en Organisatie [Financial Control and Organization]*. Alphen aan de Rijn, The Netherlands: Samson, 2015/12015/18.

Bell, J.H.J. & P.K. Jagersma. 1996. The strategic behaviour of Dutch multinational enterprises towards international joint ventures: A multidimensional analysis. In R.E. Pitts & A.G. Woodside (eds.). *Creating and managing international joint ventures*. Westport, CT: Greenwood Publishing Group.

Benito, G.R.G. 1996. Ownership structures of Norwegian foreign subsidiaries in manufacturing. *International Trade Journal*, forthcoming.

Benito, G.R.G. & G. Gripsrud. 1992. The expansion of foreign direct investments: Discrete rational location choices or a cultural learning process? *Journal of International Business Studies*, 23(3): 461-476.

Benito, G.R.G. & L.S. Welch. 1994. Foreign market servicing: Beyond choice of entry mode. *Journal of International Marketing*, 2(2): 7-27.

Berg, S.V., J.L. Duncan Jr. & P. Friedman. 1982. *Joint venture strategies and corporate innovation*. Cambridge, MA: Oelschlager, Gunn & Hain.

Bilkey, W.L. 1978. An attempted integration of the literature on the export behaviour of firms. *Journal of International Business Studies*, 9(Spring/Summer): 33-46.

Bilkey, W.J. & G. Tesar. 1977. The export behaviour of smaller Wisconsin manufacturing firms. *Journal of International Business Studies*, 8(Spring/Summer): 93-98.

Bivens, D.K. & E.B. Lovell. 1966. *Joint ventures with foreign partners*. New York: The National Conference Board.

Blodgett, L.L. 1992. Factors in the instability of international joint ventures: An event history analysis. *Strategic Management Journal*, 13: 475-481.

Boddewyn, J.J. 1985. Theories of foreign direct investment: A classificatory note. *Management International Review*, 25(1): 57-65.

Bollen, K.A. 1989. *Structural equations with latent variables*. New York: John Wiley & Sons.

Brickley, J.A. & F.H. Dark. 1987. The choice of organizational form: The case of franchising. *Journal of Financial Economics*, 18: 401-420.

Brown, L.T., A.M. Rugman & A. Verbeke. 1989. Japanese joint ventures with western multinationals: Synthesising the economic and cultural explanations of failure. *Asia Pacific Journal of Management*, 6(2): 225-242.

Brouthers, K.D., L.E. Brouthers, S. Werner & D-N. Lascu. 1993. *An integrating model of international entry mode selection: The case of the computer software industry*. Paper presented at the 1993 AIB Annual Meeting in Hawaii.

Buckley, P.J. 1983. New theories of international business: Some unresolved issues. In M. Casson (ed.). *The growth of international business*. London: George Allen & Unwin, 34-50.

Buckley, P.J. 1988. The limits of explanation: Testing the internalization theory of the multinational enterprise. *Journal of International Business Studies*, 19(2): 181-93.

Buckley, P.J. 1990. Problems and developments in the core theory of international business. *Journal of International Business Studies*, 21: 657-665.

Buckley, P.J. & M. Casson. 1976. *The future of the multinational enterprise*. London: Macmillan.

Buckley, P.J. & M. Casson (eds.). 1985. *The economic theory of the multinational enterprise*. New York: St. Martin's Press.

Buckley, P.J. & M. Casson. 1988. A theory of cooperation in international business. In F.J. Contractor & P. Lorange (eds.). *Cooperative strategies in international business*. Lexington, MA: Lexington Books, 31-55.

Buckley, P.J. & H. Davies. 1981. Foreign licensing in overseas operations: Theory and evidence from the UK. In A.G. Hawkins & A.J. Prasad (eds.). *Research in International Business and Finance*, Vol. 2. New York: JAI Press.

Bueno, A. & J. Bowditsch. 1989. *The human side of mergers and acquisitions. Managing collisions between people, cultures, and organizations*. San Francisco: Jossey-Bass.

Burgers, W.P., C.W.L. Hill & W.C. Kim. 1993. A theory of global strategic alliances: The case of the global auto industry. *Strategic Management Journal*, 14: 419-432.

Burt, R.S. 1973. Confirmatory factor analysis structures and the theory construction process. *Sociological Methods & Research*, 2: 131-187.

Byrne, B.M. 1989. *A primer of LISREL: Basic applications and programming for confirmatory factor analytic models*. New York: Springer-Verlag.

Calvet, A.L. 1981. A synthesis of foreign direct investment theories and theories of the multinational firm. *Journal of International Business Studies*, 12(Spring-Summer): 43-59.

Carter, J.R. & J. Gagne. 1988. The do's and don'ts of international countertrade. *Sloan Management Review*, 30(Spring): 31-37.

Casson, M. 1982. Transaction costs and the theory of the multinational enterprise. In A.M. Rugman (ed.). *New theories of the multinational enterprise*. London: Croom Helm.

Caves, R.E. 1971. International corporations: The industrial economics of foreign investment. *Economica*, 38(February): 1-27.

Caves, R.E. 1982. *Multinational enterprise and economic analysis*. Cambridge, MA: Cambridge University Press.

Caves, R.E. & S.K. Mehra. 1986. Entry of foreign multinationals into US manufacturing industries. In M.E. Porter (ed.). *Competition in global industries*. Boston, MA: Harvard Business School Press, 449-482.

Cavusgil, S.T. 1980. On the internationalization process of firms. *European Research*, 8 (November): 273-281.

Cavusgil, S.T. 1982. Some observations on the relevance of critical variables for internationalization stages. In M.R. Czinkota & G. Tesar (eds.). *Export management: An international context.* New York: Praeger.

Chamberlin, E.H. 1933. *The theory of monopolistic competition.* Cambridge, MA: Harvard University Press.

Cho, K.R. & P. Padmanabhan. 1995. Acquisition versus new venture: The choice of foreign establishment mode by Japanese firms. *Journal of International Management,* 1(3): 255-285.

Choudhry, Y.A., M. McGeady & R. Stiff. 1989. An analysis of attitudes of US firms towards countertrade. *Columbia Journal of World Business,* 24(Summer): 31-38.

Chowdhury, J. 1992. Performance of international joint ventures and wholly owned foreign subsidiaries: A comparative perspective. *Management International Review,* 32(2): 115-133.

Chu, W. & E. Anderson. 1992. Capturing ordinal properties of categorical dependent variables: A review with application to modes of foreign entry. *International Journal of Research in Marketing,* 9: 149-160.

Churchill, G.A. 1991. *Marketing research: Methodological foundations.* 5th. ed. Chicago: The Dryden Press.

Coase, R.H. 1937. The nature of the firm. *Economica,* 4(November): 386-405.

Cohen, W.M. & R.C. Levin. 1989. Empirical studies of innovation and market structure. In R. Schmalensee & R.D. Willig (eds.). *Handbook of industrial organization.* Volume II. Amsterdam: Elsevier Science Publishers, 1060-1107.

Cohen, W.M. & D.A. Levinthal. 1990. Absorptive capacity: A new perspective on learning and innovation. *Administrative Science Quarterly,* 35: 128-152.

Collis, D.J. 1991. A resource-based analysis of global competition: The case of the bearings industry. *Strategic Management Journal,* 12: 49-68.

Conner, K.R. 1991. A historical comparison of resource-based theory and five schools of thought within industrial organization economics: Do we have a new theory of the firm? *Journal of Management,* 17: 121-154.

Contractor, F.J. 1984. Choosing between foreign direct investment and licensing: Theoretical considerations and empirical tests. *Journal of International Business Studies,* 15: 167-188.

Contractor, F.J. 1990a. Contractual and cooperative forms of international business: Towards a unified theory of modal choice. *Management International Review,* 30(1): 31-54.

Contractor, F.J. 1990b. Ownership patterns of US joint ventures abroad and the liberalization of foreign government regulations in the 1980s: Evidence from the benchmark surveys. *Journal of International Business Studies*, 21(1): 55-73.
Contractor, F.J. & P. Lorange (eds.). 1988a. *Cooperative strategies in international business*. Lexington, MA: Lexington Books.
Contractor, F.J. & P. Lorange. 1988b. Why should firms cooperate? The strategy and economics basis for cooperative ventures. In F.J. Contractor & P. Lorange (eds.). *Cooperative strategies in international business*. Lexington, MA: Lexington Books, 3-30.
Cook, T.D. & D.T. Campbell. 1979. *Quasi-experimentation: Design and analysis issues for field settings*. Chicago: Rand McNally.
Cramer, J.S. 1991. *The logit model: An introduction for economists*. London: Edward Arnold.
Cudeck, R. 1989. Analysis of correlation matrices using covariance structure models. *Psychological Bulletin*, 105: 317-327.
Curhan, J.P., W.H. Davidson & R. Suri. 1977. *Tracing the multinationals*. Cambridge, MA: Ballinger Publishing.
Cyert, R.M. & J.G. March. 1963. *A behavioral theory of the firm*. Englewood Cliffs, N.J.: Prentice-Hall.
Czinkota, M.R. 1982. *Export development strategies: US promotion policies*. New York: Praeger Publishers.
Davidson, W.H. 1980. The location of foreign investment activity: Country characteristics and experience effects. *Journal of International Business Studies*, 11 (Fall): 9-22.
Davidson, W.H. 1982. *Global strategic management*. New York: John Wiley & Sons.
Davidson, W.H. 1983. Market similarity and market selection: Implications of international marketing strategy. *Journal of Business Research*, 11: 439-456.
Davidson W.H. & D.G. McFetridge. 1985. Key characteristics in the choice of international technology transfer mode. *Journal of International Business Studies*, 16(Summer): 5-12.
De Jong, H.W. 1985. *Dynamische markttheorie [Dynamic market theory]*. Leiden/Antwerpen: H.E. Stenfert Kroese.
DeMaris, A. 1992. *Logit modeling: Practical applications*. Sage University Paper Series on Quantitative Applications in the Social Sciences, 07-086. Newbury Park, CA: Sage Publications.
Demsetz, H. 1988. The theory of the firm revisited. *Journal of Law, Eco-nomics and Organization*, 4(1): 141-161.

Denis, J.E. & Depelteau, D. 1985. Market knowledge, diversification and export expansion. *Journal of International Business Studies*, 16: 77-89.

Dierickx, I. & K. Cool. 1989. Asset stock accumulation and sustainability of competitive advantage. *Management Science*, 35(11): 1504-1511.

Dietrich, M. 1994. *Transaction cost economics and beyond: Towards a new economics of the firm*. London: Routledge.

Dow, G.K. 1993. The appropriability critique of transaction cost economics. In C. Pitelis (ed.). *Transaction costs, markets and hierarchies*. Oxford: Blackwell.

Doz, Y. 1986. *Strategic management in multinational companies*. Oxford: Pergamon.

Dunning, J.H. 1981. *International production and the multinational enterprise*. London: Allen and Unwin.

Dunning, J.H. 1988a. *Explaining international production*. London: Unwin Hyman.

Dunning, J.H. 1988b. The eclectic paradigm of international production: A restatement and some possible extensions. *Journal of International Business Studies*, 19(Spring): 1-31.

Dunning, J.H. 1989. The theory of international production. In K. Fatemi (ed.). *International trade: Existing problems and prospective solutions*. New York: Taylor & Francis, 45-84.

Dunning, J.H. 1993. *Multinational enterprises and the global economy*. Wokingham: Addison-Wesley Publishing Company.

Dunning J.H. & A.M. Rugman. 1985. The influence of Hymer's dissertation on the theory of foreign direct investment. *American Economic Review*, 75: 228-232.

Economische Voorlichtingsdienst [Economic Information Unit]. Various years. *Vademecum voor in- en uitvoer [Handbook for import and export]*. Deventer, the Netherlands: Kluwer/Samson.

Engwall, L. & M. Wallenstål. 1988. Tit for tat in small steps: The internationalization of Swedish banks. *Scandinavian Journal of Management*, 4(3/4): 147-155.

Erramilli, M.K. 1991. The experience factor in foreign market entry behaviour of service firms. *Journal of International Business Studies*, 22(3): 479-501.

Erramilli, M.K. & C.P. Rao. 1993. Service firms' international entry mode choice: A modified transaction-cost analysis approach. *Journal of Marketing*, 57(July): 19-38.

Fagre, N. & L.T. Wells Jr. 1982. Bargaining power of multinationals and host governments. *Journal of International Business Studies*, 13(2): 9-23.

Fama, E.F. & M.C. Jensen. 1983. Separation of ownership and control. *Journal of Law and Economics*, 26: 301-326.

Financieel Economisch Lexicon [Financial Economic Lexicon]. 1993. *Dochterondernemingen en deelnemingen [Daughter firms and participations].*

Financieel Economisch Magazine [Financial Economic Magazine]. 1991.

Financieel Economisch Magazine [Financial Economic Magazine]. 1992.

Financieele Dagblad, Het [The Financial Daily]. 1993. *De omzetcijfers van 1992 [The sales of 1992].*

Ford, D. et al. 1987. Managing export development between industrialized and developing countries. In S.D. Reid & P.J. Rosson (eds.). *Managing export entry and expansion.* New York: Praeger, 71-90.

Fornell, C. & Y. Yi. 1992. Assumptions of the two-step approach to latent variable modeling. *Sociological Methods & Research*, 20(3): 291-320.

Frambach, R.T. 1993. *De adoptie en diffusie van innovaties in de industriële markt: Een empirisch onderzoek naar de verspreiding van electronic banking in Nederland [The adoption and diffusion of innovations in the industrial market: An empirical study towards the spread of electronic banking in The Netherlands].* Utrecht, the Netherlands: Uitgeverij Lemma B.V.

Francis, D. 1987. *The countertrade handbook*, Cambridge: Woodhead-Faulkner.

Franko, L.G. 1989. Use of minority and 50/50 joint ventures by United States multinationals during the 1970s: The interaction of host country policies and corporate strategies. *Journal of International Business Studies*, 20(1): 19-40.

Gatignon, H. & E. Anderson. 1988. The multinational corporation's degree of control over foreign subsidiaries: An empirical test of a transaction cost explanation. *Journal of Law, Economics, and Organization*, 4(2): 305-336.

Geringer, J.M. & L. Hebert. 1989. Control and performance of international joint ventures. *Journal of International Business Studies*, 20(2): 235-254.

Ghoshal, S. 1987. Global strategy: An organizing framework. *Strategic Management Journal*, 8: 425-440.

Gomes-Casseres, B. 1985. *Multinational ownership strategies.* Ann Arbor, MI: UMI Press (DBA dissertation).

Gomes-Casseres, B. 1987. Joint venture instability: Is it a problem? *Columbia Journal of World Business*, 22(2): 97-102.

Gomes-Casseres, B. 1989. Ownership structures of foreign subsidiaries: Theory and evidence. *Journal of Economic Behaviour and Organization*, 11: 1-25.

Gomes-Casseres, B. 1990. Firm ownership preferences and host government restrictions: An integrated approach. *Journal of International Business Studies*, 21(1): 1-22.

Goodnow, J.D. & J.E. Hanz. 1972. Environmental determinants of overseas market entry strategies. *Journal of International Business Studies*, 3: 33-50.

Grant, R.M. 1991. The resource-based theory of competitive advantage: Implications for strategy formulation. *California Management Review*, 33(3): 114-135.

Groenewegen, J. 1995. *TCE and beyond*. Boston/Deventer: Kluwer Academic Publishers.

Hagedoorn, J. 1993. Understanding the rationale of strategic technology partnering: Interorganizational modes of cooperation and sectoral differences. *Strategic Management Journal*, 14: 371-385.

Halbach, A.J. & R. Osterkamp. 1989. Countertrade with developing countries: New opportunities for North-South trade? *Intereconomics*, 24(January/February): 17-23.

Hall, R. 1992. The strategic analysis of intangible resources. *Strategic Management Journal*, 13(2): 135-144.

Hamel, G. 1991. Competition for competence and interpartner learning within international strategic alliances. *Strategic Management Journal*, 12: 83-103.

Hamel, G., Y.L. Doz & C.K. Prahalad. 1989. Collaborate with your competitors - And win. *Harvard Business Review*, 67(1): 133-139.

Harrigan, K.R. 1985a. *Strategies for joint ventures*. Lexington, MA: Lexington Books.

Harrigan, K.R. 1985b. Vertical integration and corporate strategy. *Academy of Management Journal*, 28(2): 397-425.

Harrigan, K.R. 1985c. *Strategic flexibility: A management guide for changing times*. Lexington, MA: Lexington Books.

Harrigan, K.R. 1986. *Managing for joint venture success*. Lexington, MA: Lexington Books.

Harrigan, K.R. 1988a. Joint ventures and competitive strategy. *Strategic Management Journal*, 9: 141-158.

Harrigan, K.R. 1988b. Strategic alliances and partner asymmetries. In F.J. Contractor & P. Lorange (eds.). *Cooperative strategies in international business*. Lexington, MA: Lexington Books, 205-226.

Hedlund, G. & A. Kverneland. 1985. Are strategies for foreign markets changing? The case of Swedish investment in Japan. *International Studies of Management & Organization*, XV(2): 41-59.

Hedlund, G. & A. Kverneland. 1986. Why is there so little foreign direct investment in Japan? A review of Swedish companies' experience. *Advances in International Management*, 1: 47-68.

Helleloid, D. 1992. *A resource-based theory of the multinational enterprise*. Paper presented at the 1992 EIBA Annual Meeting in Reading.

Hennart, J-F. 1982. *A theory of multinational enterprise*. Ann Arbor: University of Michigan Press.

Hennart, J-F. 1986. What is internalization? *Weltwirtschaftliches Archiv*, 122: 791-804.

Hennart, J-F. 1988. A transaction costs theory of equity joint ventures. *Strategic Management Journal*, 9: 361-374.

Hennart, J-F. 1990. Some empirical dimensions of countertrade. *Journal of International Business Studies*, 21(2): 243-270.

Hennart, J-F. 1991. The transaction costs theory of joint ventures: An empirical study of Japanese subsidiaries in the United States. *Management Science*, 37(4): 483-497.

Hennart, J-F. & Y.R. Park. 1993. Greenfield versus acquisition: The strategy of Japanese investors in the United States. *Management Science*, 39: 1054-1070.

Hennart, J-F. & Y.R. Park. 1994. Location, governance, and strategic determinants of Japanese manufacturing investment in the United States. *Strategic Management Journal*, 15: 419-436.

Hennart, J-F. & S. Reddy. 1992. *The choice between mergers/acquisitions and joint ventures: The case of Japanese investors in the United States*. Paper presented at the Workshop on Global Strategic Management Beyond the Three Generics, EIASM, Brussels.

Hill, C.W.L., P. Hwang & W.C. Kim. 1990. An eclectic theory of the choice of international entry mode. *Strategic Management Journal*, 11: 117-128.

Hill, C.W.L. & G.R. Jones. 1989. *Strategic management theory*. Boston, MA: Houghton-Mifflin.

Hill, C.W.L. & W.C. Kim. 1988. Searching for a dynamic theory of the multinational enterprise: A transaction cost model. *Strategic Management Journal*, 9(Special Issue): 93-104.

Hoekman, J.M. 1984. *The role of the joint venture in the strategy of corporations*. University of Amsterdam, Amsterdam, The Netherlands (Ph.D. dissertation).

Hofstede, G. 1980. *Culture's consequences: International differences in work-related values*. Beverly Hills, CA: Sage Publications.

Hofstede, G. 1991. *Cultures and organizations: Software of the mind.* Berkshire, England: McGraw-Hill.

Hoppe, M.H. 1990. *A comparative study of country elites: International differences in work-related values and learning and their implications for international management training and development.* University of North Carolina at Chapel Hill (unpublished Ph.D. thesis).

Horaguchi, H. & B. Toyne. 1990. Setting the record straight: Hymer, internalization theory and transaction cost economics. *Journal of International Business Studies*, 21(3): 487-494.

Hout, T., M.E. Porter & E. Rudden. 1982. How global companies win out. *Harvard Business Review*, 60(September-October): 98-108.

Hymer, S.H. 1960 & 1976. *The international operations of national firms: A study of direct foreign investment.* Cambridge, MA: MIT Press.

Hymer, S.H. 1968. La grande 'corporation' multinationale: Analyse de certaines raisons qui poussent à l'intégration internationale des affaires. *Revue Economique*, 14(6): 949-973.

Hymer, S.H. 1970. The efficiency (contradictions) of multinational corporations. *American Economic Review, Proceedings*, 441-448.

IMF. Various years. *Annual report: Exchange arrangements and exchange restrictions.*

IMF. Various years. *Annual report: Exchange restrictions.*

IMF. Various years. *Exchange arrangements and exchange restrictions.*

Ishii-Kuntz, M. 1994. *Ordinal log-linear models.* Sage University Paper Series on Quantitative Applications in the Social Sciences, 07-097. Newbury Park, CA: Sage Publications.

Itaki, M. 1991. A critical assessment of the eclectic theory of the multinational enterprise. *Journal of International Business Studies*, 22(3): 445-460.

Johanson, J. & D.D. Sharma. 1987. Technical consultancy in internationalization. *International Marketing Review*, 4: 20-29.

Johanson, J. & J.-E. Vahlne. 1977. The internationalization process of the firm: A model of knowledge development and increasing foreign market commitments. *Journal of International Business Studies*, 8(Spring/Summer): 23-32.

Johanson, J. & J.-E. Vahlne. 1990. The mechanism of internationalization. *International Marketing Review*, 7(4): 11-24.

Johanson, J. & F. Wiedersheim-Paul. 1975. The internationalization of the firm: Four Swedish cases. *Journal of Management Studies*, 12(3): 305-322.

Johnson, G. & K. Scholes. 1989. *Exploring corporate strategy.* London: Prentice Hall.

Johnston, J. 1984. *Econometric methods*. New York: McGraw-Hill.
Jöreskog, K.G. & D. Sörbom. 1988. *PRELIS, a program for multivariate data screening and data summarization*. 2nd. ed. Uppsala: University of Uppsala.
Jöreskog, K.G. & D. Sörbom. 1989. *LISREL VII user's reference guide*. Scientific Software Inc.
Kay, N.M. 1992. Markets, false hierarchies and the evolution of the modern corporation. *Journal of Economic Behaviour and Organization*, 17: 315-333.
Killing, J.P. 1980. Technology acquisition: License agreement or joint venture. *Columbia Journal of World Business*, (Fall): 38-46.
Killing, J.P. 1983. *Strategies for joint venture success*. New York: Praeger.
Kim, W.C. & P. Hwang. 1992. Global strategy and multinationals' entry mode choice. *Journal of International Business Studies*, 23(1): 29-53.
Kindleberger, C.P. 1969. *American business abroad: Six lectures on direct investment*. New Haven: Yale University Press.
Klein, S., G.L. Frazier & V.J. Roth. 1990. A transaction cost analysis model of channel integration in international markets. *Journal of Marketing Research*, 27(2): 196-208.
Kobrin, S. 1987. Testing the bargaining hypotheses in the manufacturing sector in developing countries. *International Organization*, (Autumn): 609-638.
Kogut, B. 1988. Joint ventures: Theoretical and empirical perspectives. *Strategic Management Journal*, 9: 319-332.
Kogut, B. & H. Singh. 1988a. The effect of national culture on the choice of entry mode. *Journal of International Business Studies*, 19(3): 411-432.
Kogut, B. & H. Singh. 1988b. Entering the United States by joint venture: Competitive rivalry and industry structure. In F.J. Contractor & P. Lorange (eds.). *Cooperative strategies in international business*. Lexington, MA: Lexington Books, 241-251.
Kojima, K. 1978. *Direct foreign investment: A Japanese model of multinational business operations*. London: Croom Helm.
Kojima, K. 1982. Macroeconomic versus international business approach to foreign direct investment. *Hitosubashi Journal of economics*, 23: 630-640.
Kojima, K. & T. Ozawa. 1984. Micro and macroeconomic models of foreign direct investment: Towards a synthesis. *Hitosubashi Journal of economics*, 25(2): 1-20.

Larimo, J. 1993. *Foreign direct investment behaviour and performance: An analysis of Finnish direct manufacturing investments in OECD countries*. Acta Wasaensia, no. 32. Vaasa, Finland: University of Vaasa.

Lecraw, D.J. 1984. Bargaining power, ownership, and profitability of transnational corporations in developing countries. *Journal of International Business Studies*, 15(2): 27-43.

Lecraw, D.J. 1988. Countertrade: A form of cooperative international business arrangement. In F.J. Contractor & P. Lorange (eds.). *Cooperative strategies in international business*. Lexington, MA: Lexington Books, 425-442.

Lecraw, D.J. 1989. The management of countertrade: Factors influencing success. *Journal of International Business Studies*, 20(1): 41-59.

Lessard, D.R. 1976. World, country and industry relations in equity returns: Implications for risk reduction through international diversification. *Financial Analysts Journal*, 32: 32-38.

Lessard, D.R. 1982. Multinational diversification and direct foreign investment. In D.K. Eiteman & A. Stonehill (eds.). *Multinational business finance*. Reading, MA: Addison-Wesley.

Levitt, T. 1983. The globalization of markets. *Harvard Business Review*, 61(May-June): 92-102.

Levitt, B. & J.G. March. 1988. Organizational learning. *Annual Review of Sociology*, 14: 319-340.

Li, J. 1995. Foreign entry and survival: Effects of strategic choices on performance in international markets. *Strategic Management Journal*, 16: 333-351.

Liao, T.F. 1994. *Interpreting probability models: Logit, probit, and other generalized linear models*. Sage University Paper Series on Quantitative Applications in the Social Sciences, 07-101. Newbury Park, CA: Sage Publications.

Lim, J-S., T.W. Sharkey & K.I. Kim. 1991. An empirical test of an export adoption model. *Management International Review*, 31(1): 51-62.

Little, R.J.A. & D.A. Rubin. 1987. *Statistical analysis with missing data*. New York: John Wiley & Sons.

Long, J.S. 1983a. *Confirmatory factor analysis: A preface to LISREL*. Sage University Paper Series on Quantitative Applications in the Social Sciences, 07-033. Newbury Park, CA: Sage Publications.

Long, J.S. 1983b. *Covariance structure models: An introduction to LISREL*. Sage University Paper Series on Quantitative Applications in the Social Sciences, 07-034. Newbury Park, CA: Sage Publications.

Lorange, P. & J. Roos. 1991. Why some strategic alliances succeed and others fail. *The Journal of Business Strategy*, (January/February): 25-30.

Lorange, P. & J. Roos. 1992. *Strategic alliances: Formation, implementation and evolution*. Cambridge, MA: Blackwell Publishers.

Luostarinen, R. 1980. *Internationalization of the firm*. Helsinki: The Helsinki School of Economics.

Lyles, M.A. 1988. Learning among joint venture-sophisticated firms. In F.J. Contractor & P. Lorange (eds.). *Cooperative strategies in international business*. Lexington, MA: Lexington Books, 301-316.

Madhok, A. 1994. *Mode of foreign market entry: An empirical investigation of transaction costs and organizational capability perspectives*. University of Utah, USA (mimeo).

Madhok, A. forthcoming. Cost, value and foreign market entry mode: The transaction and the firm. *Strategic Management Journal*.

Mahoney, J.T. & J.R. Pandian. 1992. The resource-based view within the conversation of strategic management. *Strategic Management Journal*, 13: 363-380.

March, J.G. 1991. Exploration and exploitation in organizational learning. *Organization Science*, 2: 71-87.

Mariti, P. & R.H. Smiley. 1983. Cooperative agreements and the organization of industry. *Journal of Industrial Economics*, (June): 437-451.

McManus, J. 1972. The theory of the international firm. In G. Paquet (ed.). *The multinational firm and the nation state*. Toronto: Collier, Macmillan, 66-93.

McVey, T.B. 1980. Countertrade and barter: Alternative trade financing by Third World Nations. *International Trade Law Journal*, 6: 197-220.

Melin, L. 1992. Internationalization as a strategy process. *Strategic Management Journal*, 13: 99-118.

Menard, S. 1995. *Applied logistic regression analysis*. Sage University Paper Series on Quantitative Applications in the Social Sciences, 07-106. Newbury Park, CA: Sage Publications.

Mintzberg, H. 1973. *The nature of managerial work*. New York: Harper & Row.

Mirus, R. & B. Yeung. 1986. Economic incentives for countertrade. *Journal of International Business Studies*, 17(Fall): 27-39.

Mirus, R. & B. Yeung. 1987. Countertrade and foreign exchange shortages: A preliminary assessment. *Weltwirtschaftliches Archiv*, 123: 535-544.

Mody, A. 1993. Learning through alliances. *Journal of Economic Behaviour and Organization*, 20: 151-170.

Moon, H.C. 1992. *A revised framework of global strategy: Extending*

the coordination-configuration framework. University of the Pacific, Stockton, CA. (mimeo).
Moon, H.C. 1993. The dynamics of Porter's three generics in international business strategy. In A.M. Rugman & A. Verbeke (eds.). *Research in global strategic management: Beyond Porter*. Greenwich, CT: JAI Press, 51-64.
Morrison, D.G. 1969. On the interpretation of discriminant analysis. *Journal of Marketing Research*, VI(May): 156-163.
Nanhekhan, R. 1990. *Cultuurverschillen gemeten: Aanknopingspunten voor wederzijds begrip tussen Nederlanders en Surinamers op de werkvloer [Cultural differences measured: Starting points for mutual comprehension between Dutch and Surinam people on the workfloor]*. Free University, Amsterdam, The Netherlands (unpublished master thesis).
Nelson, R.R. & S.G. Winter. 1982. *An evolutionary theory of economic change*. Cambridge, MA: Bellknap/Harvard.
Newbould, G.D., P.J. Buckley & J. Thurwell. 1978. *Going international: The experience of smaller companies overseas*. London: Associated Business Press.
Noorderhaven, N.G. 1994. Transaction cost analysis and the explanation of hybrid vertical inter-firm relations. *Review of Political Economy*, 6: 19-36.
Noorderhaven, N.G. 1995. *Strategic decision making*. Wokingham: Addison-Wesley Publishing Company.
Nordström, K. 1991. *The internationalization process of the firm. Searching for new patterns and explanations*. Institute of International Business, Stockholm School of Economics, Stockholm (Ph.D. dissertation).
Norušis, M.J. 1990. *SPSS/PC+ advanced statistics 4.0*. Chicago: SPSS Inc.
Nunnally, J.C. 1978. *Psychometric theory*. 2nd. ed. New york: McGraw-Hill.
OECD. 1985. *Countertrade: Developing country practices*. OECD, Paris.
OECD. 1991. *OECD economic surveys: Hungary*. OECD, Paris.
OECD. 1992. *OECD economic surveys: Poland*. OECD, Paris.
OECD. 1992. *OECD economic surveys: The Czech and Slovak Republic*. OECD, Paris.
Ohmae, K. 1985. *The triad power: The coming shape of global competition*. New York: The Free Press.

Osborn, R.N. & C.C. Baughn. 1990. Forms of interorganizational governance for multinational alliances. *Academy of Management Journal*, 33(3): 503-519.

Ouchi, W.G. 1977. The relationship between organizational structure and organizational control. *Administrative Science Quarterly*, 22: 92-112.

Padmanabhan, P. & K.R. Cho. 1994. *Ownership strategy for a foreign affiliate: An empirical investigation of Japanese firms*. Paper presented at the 1994 AIB Annual Meeting in Boston.

Parry, T. 1985. Internalization as a general theory of foreign direct investment: A critique. *Weltwirtschaftliches Archiv*, 121: 564-569.

Pennings, J.M., H.G. Barkema & S.W. Douma. 1994. Organizational learning and diversification. *Academy of Management Journal*, 37(3): 608-640.

Penrose, E. 1959. *The theory of the growth of the firm*. London: Basil Blackwell.

Perrow, C. 1986. *Complex organizations: A critical essay*. New York: McGraw-Hill.

Peteraf, M.A. 1993. The cornerstones of competitive advantage: A resource-based view. *Strategic Management Journal*, 14: 179-191.

Pfeffer, J. & G. Salancik. 1978. *The external control of organizations: A resource dependency perspective*. New York: Harper and Row.

Polanyi, M. 1967. *The tacit dimension*. New York: Doubleday.

Porter, M.E. 1980. *Competitive strategy: Techniques for analysing industries and competitors*. New York: The Free Press.

Porter, M.E. 1985. *Competitive advantage*. New York: The Free Press.

Porter, M.E. (ed.). 1986. *Competition in global industries*. Boston, MA: Harvard Business School Press.

Porter, M.E. 1987. From competitive advantage to corporate strategy. *Harvard Business Review*, 65(May-June): 43-59.

Porter, M.E. & M.B. Fuller. 1986. Coalitions and global strategies. In M.E. Porter (ed.). *Competition in global industries*. Boston, MA: Harvard Business School Press, 315-344.

Prahalad, C.K. & G. Hamel. 1990. The core competence of the corporation. *Harvard Business Review*, 68(3): 79-91.

Reich, R.B. & E.D. Mankin. 1986. Joint ventures with Japan give away our future. *Harvard Business Review*, 64(March-April): 78-86.

Richardson, G.B. 1972. The organization of industry. *Economic Journal*, 82: 883-896.

Riordan, M.H. & O.E. Williamson. 1985. Asset specificity and economic organization. *International Journal of Industrial Organization*, 3: 365-378.

Robins, J.A. 1987. Organizational economics: Notes on the use of transaction-cost theory in the study of organizations. *Administrative Science Quarterly*, 32: 68-86.
Robinson, J. 1933. *Economics of imperfect competition*. Cambridge, UK: University of Cambridge Press.
Ronen, S. & O. Shenkar. 1985. Clustering countries on attitudinal dimensions: A review and synthesis. *Academy of Management Review*, 10(3): 435-454.
Root, F.R. 1987. *Entry strategies for international markets*. Lexington, MA: Lexington Books.
Root, F.R. 1988. Environmental risks and the bargaining power of multinational corporations. *International Trade Journal*, (Fall): 111-124.
Roth, K. & A.J. Morrison. 1990. An empirical analysis of the integration-responsiveness framework in global industries. *Journal of International Business Studies*, 21(4): 541-564.
Rubin, P.H. 1973. The expansion of firms. *Journal of Political Economy*, 81: 936-949.
Rugman, A.M. 1975. Motives for foreign investment: The market imperfections and risk diversification hypothesis. *Journal of World Trade Law*, 9(September-October): 567-573.
Rugman, A.M. 1979. *International diversification and the multinational enterprise*. Lexington, MA: Lexington Books.
Rugman, A.M. 1981. *Inside the multinationals: The economics of internal markets*. London: Croom Helm.
Rugman, A.M. 1982. Internalization and non-equity forms of international involvement. In A.M. Rugman (ed.). *New theories of the multinational enterprise*. London: Croom Helm, 9-23.
Rugman, A.M. 1985. Internalization is still a general theory of foreign direct investment. *Weltwirtschaftliches Archiv*, 121: 570-575.
Rugman A.M. 1986. New theories of the multinational enterprise: An assessment of internalization theory. *Bulletin of Economic Research*, 38: 101-118.
Rugman, A.M. & A. Verbeke. 1990. *Global corporate strategy and trade policy*. London and New York: Routledge.
Rugman, A.M. & A. Verbeke. 1992. A note on the transnational solution and the transaction cost theory of multinational strategic management. *Journal of International Business Studies*, 23(4): 761-771.
Rugman, A.M. & A. Verbeke. (eds.) 1993a. *Research in global strategic management: Beyond Porter*. Greenwich, CT: JAI Press.

Rugman, A.M. & A. Verbeke. 1993b. Generic strategies in global competition. In A.M. Rugman & A. Verbeke (eds.). *Research in global strategic management: Beyond Porter.* Greenwich, CT: JAI Press, 3-16.

SAS. 1991. *SAS users guide: Procedures.* Durham, NC: The SAS Institute.

Schaan, J.L. 1988. How to control a joint venture even as a minority partner. *Journal of General Management*, 14(1): 4-16.

Schmalensee, R. 1989. Inter-industry studies of structure and performance. In R. Schmalensee & R.D. Willig (eds.). *Handbook of industrial organization.* Volume II. Amsterdam: Elsevier Science Publishers, 952-1009.

Schumpeter, J.A. 1934. *The theory of economic development.* Cambridge, MA: Harvard University Press.

Shane, S.A. 1993. The effect of cultural differences in perceptions of transactions costs on national differences in the preference for international joint ventures. *Asia Pacific Journal of Management*, 10(1): 57-69.

Shane, S.A. 1994. The effect of national culture on the choice between licensing and direct foreign investment. *Strategic Management Journal*, 15: 627-642.

Shetty, Y.K. 1979. Managing the multinational corporation: European and American styles. *Management International Review*, 19(3): 39-48.

Stalk Jr., G. 1988. Time - next source of competitive advantage. *Harvard Business Review*, 66(4): 41-51.

Stalk Jr., G., P. Evans & L.E. Shulman. 1992. Competing on capabilities: The new rules of corporate strategy. *Harvard Business Review*, 70(2): 57-69.

Stopford, J.M. & L.T. Wells Jr. 1972. *Managing the multinational enterprise: Organization of the firm and ownership of the subsidiaries.* New York: Basic Books.

Sullivan, D. & A. Bauerschmidt. 1990. Incremental internationalization: A test of Johanson and Vahlne's thesis. *Management International Review*, 30(1): 19-30.

Tallman, S.B. 1991. Strategic management models and resource-based strategies among MNEs in a host market. *Strategic Management Journal*, 12: 69-82.

Tallman, S.B. & O. Shenkar. 1994. A managerial decision model of international cooperative venture formation. *Journal of International Business Studies*, 25(1): 91-115.

Teece, D.J. 1976. *The multinational corporation and the resource cost of international technology.* Cambridge, MA: Ballinger.

Teece, D.J. 1981. The multinational enterprise: Market failure and market power considerations. *Sloan Management Review*, 22: 3-17.

Teece, D.J. 1985. Multinational enterprise, internal governance, and industrial organization. *American Economic Review*, 75(2): 233-237.

Teece, D.J. 1986. Transaction cost economics and the multinational enterprise: An assessment. *Journal of Economic Behaviour and Organization*, 7: 21-45.

Terpstra, V. & R. Sarathy. 1991. *International Marketing*. 5th. ed. New York: The Dryden Press.

Terpstra, V. & C-M. J. Yu. 1988. Determinants of foreign investment of US advertising agencies. *Journal of International Business Studies*, 19(1): 33-46.

Toyne, B. 1989. International exchange: A foundation for theory building in international business. *Journal of International Business Studies*, 20: 1-17.

Toyo Keizai Shinposha. 1987. *Japanese overseas investments, 1985-86*. Tokyo, Toyo Keizai Shinposha.

Toyo Keizai Shinposha. 1992. *Japanese overseas investments: A complete listing by firms and countries, 1992-93*. Tokyo, Toyo Keizai Shinposha.

Tschoegl, A.E. 1982. Foreign bank entry into Japan and California. In A.M. Rugman (ed.). *New theories of the multinational enterprise*. London: Croom Helm, 196-216.

Turnbull, P.W. 1987. A challenge to the stages theory of the internationalization process. In P.J. Rosson & S.D. Reid (eds.). *Managing export entry and expansion*. New York: Praeger, 21-40.

UNCTC. Various years. *National legislation and regulations relating to transnational corporations*. New York.

Unesco. Various years. *Statistical Yearbook*.

Unesco. 1990. *Compendium of statistics on illiteracy*. no. 31.

United Nations. 1992. *World investment directory 1992: Foreign direct investment, legal framework and corporate data. Volume II: Central and Eastern Europe*. New York.

Varga, K. 1986. *Az emberi és szervezeti erőforrás fejlesztése*. Budapest: Akadémiai Kiadó.

Vernon, R. 1966. International investment and international trade in the product cycle. *Quarterly Journal of Economics*, 80: 190-207.

Vernon, R. 1977. *Storm over the multinationals*. Cambridge: Harvard University Press.

Vernon, R. 1979. The product cycle hypothesis in the new international environment. *Oxford Bulletin of Economics and Statistics*, 41: 255-267.

Walker, G. & D. Weber. 1984. A transaction cost approach to make-or-buy decisions. *Administrative Science Quarterly*, 29: 373-391.
Welch, L.S. 1990. Internationalization by Australian franchisers. *Asia Pacific Journal of Management*, 7(2): 101-121.
Welch, L.S. & R. Luostarinen. 1988. Internationalization: Evolution of a concept. *Journal of General Management*, 14(2): 34-55.
Wernerfelt, B. 1984. A resource-based view of the firm. *Strategic Management Journal*, 5: 171-180.
Westney, D.E. 1988. Domestic and foreign learning curves in managing international cooperative strategies. In F.J. Contractor & P. Lorange (eds.). *Cooperative strategies in international business*. Lexington, MA: Lexington Books, 339-346.
Williamson, O.E. 1975. *Markets and hierarchies*. New York: The Free Press.
Williamson, O.E. 1979. Transaction cost economics: The governance of contractual relations. *Journal of Law and Economics*, 22(2): 223-261.
Williamson, O.E. 1981. The modern corporation: Origins, evolution, attributes. *Journal of Economic Literature*, 19(December): 1537-1568.
Williamson, O.E. 1985. *The economic institutions of capitalism*. New York: The Free Press.
Williamson, O.E. 1991a. Comparative economic organization: The analysis of discrete structural alternatives. *Administrative Science Quarterly*, 36: 269-296.
Williamson, O.E. 1991b. Strategizing, economizing, and economic organization. *Strategic Management Journal*, 12(Special Issue): 75-94.
Williamson, O.E. 1992. Markets, hierarchies, and the modern corporation: An unfolding perspective. *Journal of Economic Behaviour and Organization*, 17: 335-352.
Williamson, O.E. 1993. Opportunism and its critics. *Managerial and Decision Economics*, 14: 97-107.
Wilson, B.D. 1980. The propensity of multinational companies to expand through acquisitions. *Journal of International Business Studies*, 11(Spring/Summer): 59-65.
Wind, Y. & H.V. Perlmutter. 1977. On the identification of the frontier issues of international marketing. *Columbia Journal of World Business*, 12(Winter): 131.
Woodcock, C.P., P.W. Beamish & S. Makino. 1994. Ownership-based entry mode strategies and international performance. *Journal of International Business Studies*, 25(2), 253-273.
World Bank. 1993. *World Tables 1992*.
Yin, R.K. 1989. *Case study research: Design and methods*. Newbury Park, CA: Sage.

Yip, G. 1982. *Barriers to entry*. Lexington, MA: Lexington Books.

Yu, C-M. J. 1990. The experience effect and foreign direct investment. *Weltwirtschaftliches Archiv*, 126(3): 561-580.

Zejan, M. 1990. New ventures or acquisitions: The choice of Swedish multinational enterprises. *Journal of Industrial Economics*, 38: 349-355.